POPULAR DAY HIKES

Northern Okanagan

VERNON | SHUSWAP | LUMBY

GERRY SHEA

RMB

Copyright © 2019 by Gerry Shea
First Revised and Updated Edition
Originally published in 2013 as *Popular Day Hikes 3: Northern Okanagan*

For information on purchasing bulk quantities of this book, or to obtain media excerpts or invite the author to speak at an event, please visit rmbooks.com and select the "Contact" tab.

RMB | Rocky Mountain Books Ltd.
rmbooks.com
@rmbooks
facebook.com/rmbooks

Cataloguing data available from Library and Archives Canada
ISBN 9781771602457 (paperback)
ISBN 9781771602761 (electronic)

Printed and bound in Canada by Friesens

We would like to also take this opportunity to acknowledge the traditional territories upon which we live and work. In Calgary, Alberta, we acknowledge the Niitsitapi (Blackfoot) and the people of the Treaty 7 region in Southern Alberta, which includes the Siksika, the Piikuni, the Kainai, the Tsuut'ina and the Stoney Nakoda First Nations, including Chiniki, Bearpaw, and Wesley First Nations. The City of Calgary is also home to Métis Nation of Alberta, Region III. In Victoria, British Columbia, we acknowledge the traditional territories of the Lkwungen (Esquimalt, and Songhees), Malahat, Pacheedaht, Scia'new, T'Sou-ke and W̱SÁNEĆ (Pauquachin, Tsartlip, Tsawout, Tseycum) peoples.

We acknowledge the financial support of the Government of Canada through the Canada Book Fund and the Canada Council for the Arts, and of the province of British Columbia through the British Columbia Arts Council and the Book Publishing Tax Credit.

Disclaimer

The actions described in this book may be considered inherently dangerous activities. Individuals undertake these activities at their own risk. The information put forth in this guide has been collected from a variety of sources and is not guaranteed to be completely accurate or reliable. Many conditions and some information may change owing to weather and numerous other factors beyond the control of the authors and publishers. Individuals or groups must determine the risks, use their own judgment, and take full responsibility for their actions. Do not depend on any information found in this book for your own personal safety. Your safety depends on your own good judgment based on your skills, education, and experience.

It is up to the users of this guidebook to acquire the necessary skills for safe experiences and to exercise caution in potentially hazardous areas. The authors and publishers of this guide accept no responsibility for your actions or the results that occur from another's actions, choices, or judgments. If you have any doubt as to your safety or your ability to attempt anything described in this guidebook, do not attempt it.

Contents

Area Map   4
Introduction   5
Using this Book   8

Vernon

1. Bluenose Mountain   10
2. BX Creek Falls   13
3. Comin' Round the Mountain   16
4. Cosens Bay   19
5. Cougar Canyon   22
6. Ravine Edge   26
7. Enderby Cliffs   29
8. Mounts Rose and Swanson   32
9. Grey Canal Trail   36
10. Oyama Lookout   40
11. Rimrocks   43
12. Shorts Creek Canyon Rim   46
13. Fintry Falls   50
14. Sugarloaf Mountain   55

Lumby

15. Eagle Crest Cliffs   58
16. Rawlings Lake Cliffs   62
17. Denison Lake   66

North Shuswap

18. Adams River Trail to Adams River
    Gorge   69
19. Lower Flume Trail   72
20. Upper Flume Trail   75
21. Tsútswecw Provincial Park   79

South Shuswap

22. Fly Hills Recreation Area Lookout   83
23. Hyde Mountain Lookout   87
24. Larch Hills Nordic Trail Centre   91
25. South Canoe Trail System   94
26. Park Hill Trail System Outer Loop   97
27. Little Mountain Park   101
28. Salmon Arm Waterfront Trail
    (including Salmon Arm Wharf Trail
    and Raven Trail)   104
29. Margaret Falls   109
30. Margaret Falls Upper Canyon
    Loop   113
31. Reinecker Creek Lower Loop   116
32. Sunnybrae Bluffs   119
33. Skimikin Lake Recreation Area –
    Mount Hilliam South Slope Loop   122
34. Skimikin Lake Recreation Area –
    East View Loop   128
35. Skimikin Lake to Granite Creek
    Estate Winery   131
36. Tappen Bluffs   134
37. Balmoral Lookout Loop   137
38. Blind Bay to White Lake
    Connector   139
39. Blind Bay Lookout   142

Useful websites   144
Acknowledgements   144

Area Map

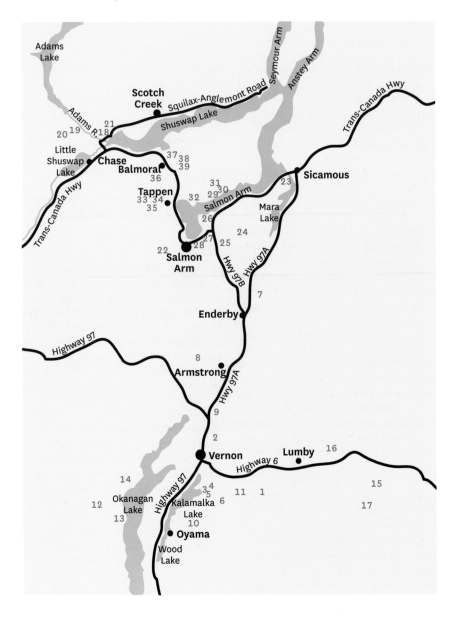

Introduction

About the North Okanagan Valley

Stretching north to south in south-central British Columbia, the Okanagan Valley is almost 200 km long, with an average width of 20 km. Lying between the Cascade and Columbia mountain ranges, the North Okanagan Valley extends from Vernon to the Shuswap, including Salmon Arm, Sicamous and Scotch Creek. In this region, the Monashee Mountains are the prominent subrange of the Columbia Mountains.

Known for its climate, and enjoying consequent popularity as a summer playground, the region has lakes that are plentiful and large, characterized by an oblong shape which is generally the result of glacial advancement and retreat. This same glacial activity has created exceedingly deep lakes, with Adams Lake being the second deepest in British Columbia (the deepest being Quesnel Lake).

The soil of the North Okanagan is mainly a mixture of sand, silt and gravel, resulting in fertile land for farming. With annual precipitation of only 410 mm, and average summer temperatures of 27.3°C with 304 days of sunshine, the Okanagan Valley is the richest, most diverse and productive agricultural zone in British Columbia after the Fraser Valley. Winters are mild, and although the snow can fall with ferocity, it doesn't stay for long, so spring in the lowlands of the valley arrives early. This usually allows for a relatively timely start to the hiking season.

Classified as a semi-arid region with sparse forests and open grasslands, the North Okanagan has plentiful hiking and backpacking routes. There are dozens of parks and recreational areas and just as many provincial parks, providing ample trails with incredible views. The hills are rolling mounds with countless ridges and modest peaks. This zone is truly a day hiker's dream.

Fruit trees are not native to the Okanagan, although they are one of the most abundant species up and down the valley. The first fruit trees were planted by Hiram Smith near Osoyoos in the late 1850s. Today, crops include apple, peach, pear, plum, apricot and cherry. Indigenous forests are comprised mainly of varieties of hemlock and cedar. Intense summer heat, combined with dry air, readily burns off grasses on open hillsides by late June, leaving cactus and sagebrush to dominate the open hillsides.

Getting there

Highway 97 goes through the middle of the city of Vernon and can be accessed from Vancouver through the winding Crowsnest Highway (Highway 3), which departs from the town of Hope, heads east toward Princeton and empties into Highway 97 in the south Okanagan Valley. Travel north on Highway 97 to arrive at Vernon. Alternatively, take the Coquihalla Highway from Hope to Merritt, veering off of the Coquihalla onto Highway 97C. This will also take you to the South Okanagan. Drive north on Highway 97 to Vernon. From Vernon you can reach Armstrong and Enderby by driving farther north on Highway 97A.

To get to Vernon from Calgary, travel west on the Trans-Canada Highway and turn south at Sicamous onto Highway 97A. From Sicamous you will reach Enderby and Armstrong before arriving at Vernon.

Lumby is located 27 km east of Vernon by way of Highway 6.

Sicamous, Salmon Arm, Tappen, Balmoral and Sorrento are all situated on the Trans-Canada Highway, while the North Shuswap, Scotch Creek and Skimikin Lake Recreation Area are all accessed directly from the Trans-Canada. Refer to individual trail "Start" descriptions for precise directions.

Seasonal road closures

There are no planned seasonal highway closures through the Okanagan/Shuswap region, but inclement winter weather can create unscheduled temporary closures.

All gravel forest service roads (FSRs) are subject to late fall, winter and early spring closures, as many of them are not maintained during these times. During spring runoff, many FSRs can be closed for several weeks and some can even be washed away altogether. This has never been quite as evident as it became in the spring of 2012 when several gravel and paved roads were washed away and not repaired until mid- to late summer. Refer to the provincial website www.drivebc.ca for updates.

Facilities

Scotch Creek, Sorrento, Vernon, Salmon Arm, Lumby, Armstrong and Sicamous all have full amenities.

The west side of Okanagan Lake has limited amenities, so be sure to fuel up before leaving Vernon. Camping with full hookups is available along Westside Road, and resort accommodation is also available.

Only limited services are found along the Sunnybrae–Canoe Point road, although there are two gas stations and a convenience store in Tappen, at the entrance to the Sunnybrae area. Tappen and Sunnybrae have camping with full hookups available for overnight accommodation, but there are no hotels or motels.

The Balmoral area has a single gas station with convenience store on the Trans-Canada Highway, but full amenities can be found at Sorrento, 10 km west of Balmoral.

Weather

Summers in the North Okanagan are mild, with hot days, warm nights and low humidity. July and August weather is considered tropical with temperatures commonly reaching the mid-30s and averaging 27.3°C, with 304 days of sunshine annually. Precipitation averages about 410 mm each year.

Winters are mild, with moderate snowfall and average temperatures hovering just above 0°C. Cold snaps as low as −25°C can last for a couple of weeks at a time, but these are rare.

What does this mean for us day hikers? Despite snowpack runoff from higher elevations into the lowland, the hiking season begins in early spring in many areas. Some trails are snow free as early as March and April. Summer months obviously are dry and hot, but autumn provides cooler hiking conditions before the snow falls, allowing some late season trekking.

Drinking water

Although creeks and drainage channels are abundant during spring and early summer, most secondary water sources dry up soon after snowmelt. This creates a scarcity of drinking water during the bulk of the hiking season, so bring your water supply for the day from home, campground or motel. Even during spring runoff, when water is plentiful, bear in mind that this is an agricultural and ranching region, so the water may not be as pure as it appears. *Giardia lamblia* is the primary parasite that contaminates these waters and it can cause a variety of symptoms including diarrhea, gas or bloating, headache, nausea and a low-grade fever. Even the large lakes contain contaminants, and levels of fecal coliform can be high during the summer months as the shoreline's cabins and resorts reach capacity.

Wildlife concerns

The two foremost wildlife concerns in the Okanagan are black bears and cougars, with bears being the more common of the two. Stay alert for bears at all times; there could be one around any corner. Make noise, travel in groups and keep a sharp eye on the trail. Bears come out of hibernation in early spring, looking to fill their empty bellies with as many berries as they can find, so as you enter a clearing, or an avalanche slope, look first before going in. The best way to avoid a bear encounter is to avoid a bear encounter. Stay out of their way!

Small wildlife can also be bothersome. The hot, dry Okanagan climate is ideal for ticks, and spring is when they are at their peak. Generally their life cycle makes them a danger during April, May and June, but the tick season can occur later if spring has been excessively wet. Most ticks in the Okanagan are wood ticks and do not carry Lyme disease bacteria. Check your clothing before getting into your vehicle after a hike so you don't take any of the little critters back home with you. And don't forget to check family pets if they've been out hiking with you.

Safety tips

Carry bear spray with you at all times, even on short hikes. Bears in the Okanagan are becoming more urbanized as we encroach into their territory, so they may be closer to a roadside stroll than you might think. It is always a good idea to travel in groups, to deter curious bears and for assistance if someone should become injured or ill.

Stay on the trails. Many of the trails and forest service roads in this area skirt cliffs and ledges that have substantial drops. As well, getting caught up in gnarly rocks or windfallen trees can easily twist an ankle.

There is good cellular coverage throughout most of the hikes in this guide, so carrying a phone is good for emergencies or to ease the minds of loved ones awaiting your return should you run late. Although registration with park authorities or RCMP is not necessary for any of the trails in this guide, you should always let someone know where you are going and when you expect to return, even if you are travelling in a group. An entire group can be in danger

and out of cell range just as easily as an individual hiker.

Take a small flashlight in case you return after sunset. No matter how well you plan your hike, there are always unforeseen events that can keep you after dark.

Keep your dog on a leash. If your dog encounters a bear he will bark and chase it around long enough to put the bear into frenzy, and when this frenzy becomes too much for your dog to handle, he's going to come back to you, and guess who's going to follow him? Yes, the angry bear.

The Okanagan has regular hunting seasons in the fall (even a few minor migratory bird seasons in the summer), so wear brightly coloured clothing from mid-September on. A bright-orange hat is also a good idea in the fall. Check the Region 8 British Columbia Hunting & Trapping Regulations Synopsis for open areas before heading out (see under "Useful websites" on p. 144).

Using this Book

How the trails were chosen

This book describes day hikes throughout the North Okanagan Valley, Lumby and Shuswap Lake regions. Digging deeper into each region, the Vernon section refers to treks around Vernon, Westside Road, Enderby and Armstrong, while the Shuswap region includes Salmon Arm, Sicamous, Tappen, Sunnybrae and the North Shuswap, in particular Scotch Creek.

I have selected the most scenic and interesting trails in these entire regions. Some are riverside strolls, some are walks to the top of mountains, some will take you into the guts of canyons, and some of these trails will take you through some marvellous meadows. I have been hiking throughout the North Okanagan and Shuswap for many years and have made certain that I have selected only the best trails out of the extensive number to choose from.

My motivation for composing this book, as well as my *Aspiring Hiker's Guide* series, is simple: I love to see people out on the trail. I like to encourage people to put on their boots and get out and hike. So this book, and others that I write, are intended to encourage everyone to get off the couch and get outside and enjoy the beauty that is waiting at their doorstep.

Trails

The majority of trails in the immediate Vernon area are marked with green arrows painted on wood planks which are nailed to trees at important junctions. These trails include Rimrocks, Bluenose Mountain, Cougar Canyon, Denison Lake, Oyama Lookout, Ravine Edge, Mounts Rose and Swanson, Shorts Creek Canyon Rim and Sugarloaf Mountain.

Most of the trails in the Shuswap area are marked with metal signs screwed onto sturdy 4" × 4" posts. These trail markers are the result of hard work by the mostly volunteer Shuswap Trail Alliance. Trails constructed and maintained by this group include Hyde Mountain Lookout, South Canoe Trail System, Park Hill Trail System, Salmon Arm Waterfront Trail, Reinecker Creek Lower Loop, Comin' Round the Mountain, Cosens Bay, Balmoral to White Lake Trail, Balmoral Viewpoint and Blind Bay Lookout Trail. Corporate sponsorship also helps to keep these trails maintained and growing in numbers. The Skimikin Lake Recreation Area is kept in great shape by volunteers from a variety of equestrian and ATV clubs.

Some trail systems such as Lower and Upper Flume, Adams River, Shorts Creek Canyon Falls, Margaret Falls, Margaret Falls Upper Canyon Loop and Tsútswecw Provincial Park are maintained by the provincial government, while many others, such as Sunnybrae Lookout, Tappen Bluffs and Fly Hills Recreation Area Lookout, have no markers or directional signs whatsoever. Larch Hills Nordic Trail System and Eagle Crest Cliffs are maintained on private property and are well marked.

Many trails are multi-purpose and accommodate hikers, bikers and horses. A limited number of the trails in this book allow motorized vehicles, but I have kept your exposure to these to a minimum.

Numbered text

For ease of use and simplicity, each trek's routes have been broken down into numbered paragraphs to enable a smoother flow of direction.

Difficulty

These are day hikes, but there is significant variation from hike to hike. Some are all but level, while others are nothing short of a straight skyward climb. Consequently there is a basic grading system ranging from Easy to Strenuous. The difficulty of trails is assessed on three factors: grade; distance; and potential exposure to dangerous terrain.

Distances and definitions

All distances are listed from the trailhead to the destination as round-trip hikes. Should a particular route have the option of becoming a "Through" hike (see #1 just below), split the round-trip hike's distance in half to obtain the through distance. "Loop" hikes (#2 below) are measured from the trailhead as a single route which arcs around and returns to the same trailhead.

Height gain (where relevant) and a rough estimate of the time needed to complete a round trip are included in the header for each route. The elevation of each route's highest point is also noted.

There are three categories of hikes, with some being a combination of two categories:

1. **THROUGH**: These are routes that have a parking lot at each end. All Through hikes can also become Return hikes, of course, if you have not arranged to have a second vehicle waiting at the far end and you instead just retrace your steps to return to your starting point.

2. **LOOP**: These hikes complete a circuit, beginning and ending at the same point but not retracing your steps. Some Loop hikes will have an additional "subloop" somewhere along their route which departs from and ultimately returns to the original Loop trail.

3. **RETURN**: Usually associated with mountain summit destinations. There is only one way in and the same way back out.

Sketch maps

Trails are sketched as a succession of green dots that are highlighted with a yellow glow. Main roads and highways appear as continuous yellow lines, while secondary roads, including gravel forest service roads, are represented by a solid red line. The maps are to scale, but not detailed. The combination of map and written directions will easily guide you to each trailhead and destination.

Other maps

Canadian Topographical Maps can be used should you require more detail. Natural Resources Canada topographic mapping classification maps referenced for the North Okanagan and Shuswap are 82L02, 82L03, 82L04, 82L05, 82L06, 82L07, 82L11, 82L12, 82L13, 82L14 and 82L15.

What to wear

Dress for heat and direct sunlight in June, July and August. Temperatures readily reach and even exceed 35°C in the summer months, and with long days, heat stroke is an ever-present danger. A hat and sunscreen are also highly recommended. Short pants and wickable short-sleeved shirts will help keep you cool as well. Although the weather can change, it is not usually abrupt, but packing a light jacket or raingear is a good idea. Mosquito repellent also will help make your hiking trips much more enjoyable.

As the summer fades, the days become shorter and cooler, so dress accordingly. A heavier jacket and long pants will be more comfortable during cool autumn day hikes. Spring hiking can be damp as well as cold, so raingear is also recommended.

Light hiking boots will suffice for all routes in this book.

1 Bluenose Mountain

Bluenose Mountain actually consists of three summits, of which only two are located on public land, leaving the third one inaccessible on private property. The journey provides a walk through a forest of spruce, and the scenery from the two summits is remarkable.

The dual summits have enough distance between them to provide distinctive views of the same geographic location. The downside is that ascending two separate summits requires significant work.

CATEGORY: Loop

DISTANCE: 4.4 km round-trip

HEIGHT GAIN: 259 m

HIGH POINT: 1254 m

TIME: 1.75–2 hrs.

DIFFICULTY: Strenuous

SEASONS: Summer, fall

TRAILHEAD COORDINATES: N50 11 29.4 W119 04 22.8

DIRECTIONS TO TRAILHEAD: In Vernon, at the major intersection of Highway 97 (32nd St.) and 25th Ave., drive east, following the signs for Kalamalka Lake, Lumby, Nelson and Highway 6 South. Turn right onto Highway 6 and travel 11.3 km to Learmouth Rd. Go 5.7 km along Learmouth Rd., turn left onto Reid Rd. and follow it for 1.3 km until it turns into gravel. Reid Rd. has a few different names as it makes some sharp turns, so don't be surprised when you find yourself on Whitevale, Bluenose and finally Aberdeen roads. The end result is that the trailhead is 4.2 km from the start of the gravel, with the sign for Bluenose Trail on the left side of the road.

1. The path begins as a very steep climb in sparse forest. Fortunately, however, the local hiking club has spent substantial time and effort creating a series of switchbacks that criss-cross the direct route, making the ascent much easier. A marker on a tree will lead you to the switchbacks starting on your right. More markers (usually green arrows) keep you on the main trail. As the path zigzags slowly up the hillside, the forest gradually thins out, enabling expansive views of rolling hills, farm fields and valleys.

2. At the 1 km mark, or 15 minutes into the hike, the trail levels just prior to encountering a minor intersection. Note the arrow pointing to the right; do not continue straight as the trail might seem to indicate.

3. More upward hairpin turns keep you panting for another five minutes to where the trail briefly flattens. Another green arrow takes you off the main trail, directing you upward to the left. This diversion's destination is the first summit. Eventually you will return back down to this spot to take up the main trail to reach the third summit. Take a deep breath; although this first summit is only five minutes away, it is a sluggish grind of steep switchbacks.

4. After reaching the first summit, drop back down the same switchbacks to pick up the main trail once again and continue your way to the third summit. Remember, the second summit is inaccessible, as it's located on private property. Ten minutes of rolling up and down on a narrow path brings you to a minor summit that provides generous viewing similar to the sights from

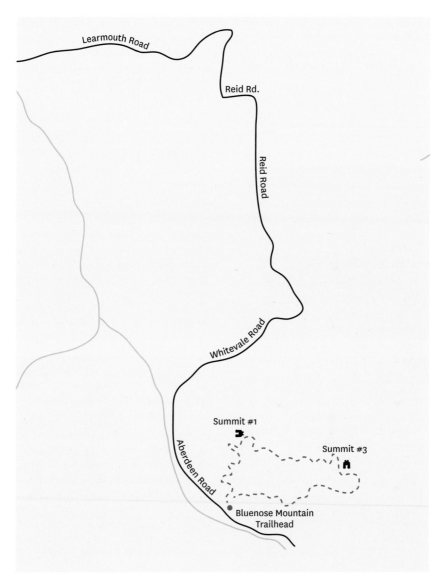

the first peak. This is not the third peak yet, though. You might want to sit awhile and enjoy the view, because you still have substantial work ahead of you.

5. Leaving this small summit, the trail begins to decline for about 10 minutes before heading skyward. The descent is through a coniferous forest shrouded in "black tree lichen," also known as wila. This dark-brown plant, resembling strands of hair, is a traditional food source for many First Nations people.

6. The walking distance between the first and third summits is only about 1.3 km, but half of that distance will take the most time: a 20-minute upward struggle of relentless

switchbacks. When the third summit is finally attained, it presents beautiful panoramas of the east and south valleys. Canyons and creekbeds, farmland and forests are in abundance.

7. Walk the short summit to the far end to continue this fabulous loop walk. The trail tumbles downhill for about 20 minutes and levels off for an additional 10 minutes to finally bring you back to your car.

TOP: *A few scattered residents dwell in the amazing landscape around Bluenose Mountain.*

BOTTOM: *The east Vernon townships of Coldstream and Lavington are easily surveyed from various points on the Bluenose Mountain hike.*

2 BX Creek Falls

This short, easy hike takes place in a dark, cool canyon, providing a chilly retreat from the blazing sun of the Okanagan. With a one-way distance of 3.2 km and limited elevation gain, this hike can easily be done as a Through route. Alternatively, there is parking at both ends of the hike. This description is a round-trip route starting and ending at the Star Rd. parking lot.

CATEGORY: Through

DISTANCE: 6 km round trip; can also be done as a Through hike

HEIGHT GAIN: Nominal

HIGH POINT: 693 m

TIME: 1.5–2 hrs. round trip

DIFFICULTY: Moderate

SEASONS: Late spring, summer, fall

TRAILHEAD COORDINATES: N50 17 49.6 W119 12 56.2

DIRECTIONS TO TRAILHEAD: Travelling north on 27th St. in Vernon, turn right onto 48th Ave. (which becomes Silver Star Rd. as it crosses Pleasant Valley Rd.). Drive 3.5 km to an intersection with Star Rd. Turn right on Star Rd. and drive 500 m to the parking lot, which will be on your right. An alternative parking lot is 2 km farther up Star Rd., with a turn right onto Tillicum Rd. This lot too is on the right.

1. Beginning at the Star Rd. parking lot, find the well-marked trailhead and begin trekking a wide, level path. Within five minutes you will come across a chain-link fence surrounding a portion of the creek to prevent wayward travellers from tumbling over a small man-made waterfall. This waterfall, spilling over concrete, is the overflow from the BX Creek sediment pond.

2. As the trail continues beyond this structure, it becomes narrow, rocky and rooty until it approaches an insignificant junction. Stay on the right-hand path. From here, the roots and rocks give way to a delightful dirt path which enters a dark, thick forest of cedar and hemlock. The path follows BX Creek all the way to the falls.

3. The trail takes occasional diversions over small bluffs, but for the most part it winds its way alongside the creek.

4. Just after the first kilometre, you come to the first of four or five bridges. Some of these bridges simply cross the creek from bank to bank, while others present stairways of landscaping ties at the opposite end.

5. At the 3 km point of the trek, the final upward stairway is a colossal achievement that rises skyward from the canyon floor. This effort takes you to fabulous viewing of BX Creek Falls.

6. If you are not yet tired of climbing stairs, there is another stairway that descends to the base of the falls for a superior view of the tumbling water exiting a chute.

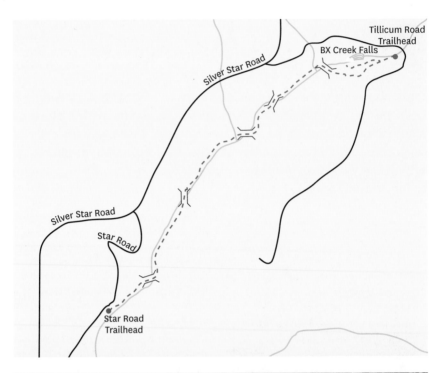

TOP: *BX Creek.*

BOTTOM: *The exit out of the BX Creek canyon is augmented with a sturdy staircase.*

OPPOSITE: *The trek to BX Creek Falls begins as a wide, level path but soon drops down into a canyon of cedar and hemlock.*

3 Comin' Round the Mountain

This journey circumnavigates many of the hiking trails of Kalamalka Lake Provincial Park. With this being an outer loop walk, vistas of Kalamalka Lake and the surrounding hills abound for most of the journey.

CATEGORY: Loop

DISTANCE: 10.5 km round trip with loop trail

HEIGHT GAIN: Nominal

HIGH POINT: 653 m

TIME: 2–2.5 hrs. round trip

DIFFICULTY: Moderate

SEASONS: Late spring, summer, fall

TRAILHEAD COORDINATES: N50 12 34.2 W119 13 56.2

DIRECTIONS TO TRAILHEAD: In Vernon, at the major intersection of Highway 97 (32nd St.) and 25th Ave., drive eastward, following the signs for Kalamalka Lake, Lumby, Nelson and Highway 6 South. Turn right onto Highway 6 and drive for less than a kilometre, looking for Kalamalka Lake Rd. Turn right on Kalamalka Lake Rd. and stay on it for a little over 6 km before turning right on Coldstream Creek Rd. Within 800 m, turn left onto Cosens Bay Rd. The parking lot is another 800 m down the road. Alternatively, follow Provincial Park signs directing you to Cosens Bay, starting at the intersection of Highway 6 and Kalamalka Lake Rd. through to the parking lot.

1. Find the trailhead at the northeast end of the parking lot to begin travelling a narrow path. Almost immediately, the trail veers upward to the left at a sign confirming the trail.

2. Moderate elevation is gained for the next 10–15 minutes. About 15 minutes from the trailhead, another sign keeps you on the correct trail. This one gives directions to The Wall up to the left, but you want to stay on the main trail, continuing straight and heading downhill.

3. All along this hike, minor trails intersect and join the main route, but staying on the core trail is straightforward.

4. The area becomes open, wide and vast about 30–35 minutes into the hike, and with this expansive view, the shimmering waters of Kalamalka Lake, down to your right, become the focal point of the hike. Five minutes later you will come to another sign, on your left, marking the trail called The Parabola. Stay on the main path, heading straight.

5. The remainder of the trail continuously heads in and out of a sparse mixed forest of pine and alders, while rolling almost unnoticeably up and down.

6. You will come to a third noteworthy junction nearly 10 minutes from The Parabola intersection. Once more, the junction approaches from the left; the sign gives the trail's name as The Lookout.

7. Almost as soon as you pass The Lookout junction, the trail dips down to join a wider, more travelled one. You will pass a sign on your left announcing that the trail you are currently on is at the beginning (or the end) of the trail called Comin' Round the Mountain. Join this new trail by turning left, putting you on Corral Trail. Its namesake is soon apparent. Corral Trail comes

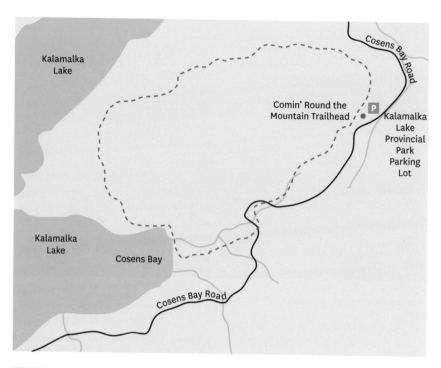

Much of the hike on the Comin' Round the Mountain circuit goes through vast green grasslands which become burnt brown by midsummer.

Glimpses soon become spectacular views as the path meanders closer to Kalamalka Lake.

up on your right from the Red Gate parking lot. The intersection of these two footpaths marks 4.3 km into the hike.

8. Continue on Corral Trail for another 15 minutes until you arrive at a fork. Grassland Trail goes down to the right, while Corral Trail is the left fork heading upward. Take Corral Trail, which ultimately takes you to Cosens Bay Beach 1.3 km away.

9. A couple of minutes up Corral Trail you'll pass a magnificent lookout just off the right side of the path. There is a comfortable, inviting bench here that encourages you to take a break and enjoy a spectacular view of Kalamalka Lake. You really should stop and take a look. Don't be in too much of a rush to get back to your car – you have all day.

10. After another two minutes or so, the trail passes another park bench to your right. At this spot, the trail takes an unannounced dip down toward the lake as it swings away from a straight, level, single-track path directly ahead of you. There are no direction signs here as you drop downward on switchbacks, but I can guarantee you this is the right way.

11. Just over 10 minutes later you will approach Sidewinder Trail and its marker on your left. Stick to the main trail, and a few minutes later you will be on Cosens Bay beach.

12. Walk the beach trail for about five minutes to find the end of Cosens Bay Trail (see the Cosens Bay hike, next, for details). As you access Cosens Bay Trail, you have trekked about 6.5 km so far.

13. Continue up Cosens Bay Trail for 3.5 km to return to your vehicle.

4 Cosens Bay

This pleasant 3 km one-way stroll through open fields to Kalamalka Lake is ideal on a hot Okanagan day. A dip in the warm waters of Kalamalka Lake is a tremendous reward for so little effort.

CATEGORY: Return

DISTANCE: 6 km round trip

HEIGHT GAIN: 152 m

HIGH POINT: 559 m

TIME: 1.5–2 hrs. round trip

DIFFICULTY: Moderate

SEASONS: Late spring, summer, fall

TRAILHEAD COORDINATES: N50 12 34.2 W119 13 56.2

DIRECTIONS TO TRAILHEAD: In Vernon, at the major intersection of Highway 97 (32nd St.) and 25th Ave., drive east, following the signs for Kalamalka Lake, Lumby, Nelson and Highway 6 South. Turn right onto Highway 6 and drive for less than a kilometre, looking for Kalamalka Lake Rd. Turn right on Kalamalka Lake Rd. and stay on it for a little over 6 km until turning right on Coldstream Creek Rd. Within 800 m, turn left onto Cosens Bay Rd., which services Kalamalka Lake Provincial Park. The parking lot is another 800 m down the road. Alternatively, follow Provincial Park signs to Cosens Bay, starting at the intersection of Highway 6 and Kalamalka Lake Rd. through to the parking lot.

1. Leaving the parking lot, the trail gently climbs briefly through sparse forest, opening to a vast meadow after just a few minutes of walking. The grasses in this broad meadow are green only for a short time during spring and early summer. By August these rolling hills of flowers and green grass will have evolved into hills of empty, burnt-brown stalks.

2. The way is obvious even with the multitude of cycle paths intersecting the main trail. Well-placed signage guides you. The "summit" of the trail is reached after about 500 m along the trail. The elevation of the summit is 559 m above sea level. Although you've gained 67 m, the trail now descends to Kalamalka Lake with a drop of 152 m.

3. From the summit, you receive your first glimpse of Kalamalka Lake as the trail begins its slow, steady descent through openness to the shores of the wondrous "lake of many colours." You cross the gravelled Cosens Bay Rd. twice as it winds its way down to the lake, having left the parking lot where the trail did. The first crossing is within five minutes of leaving the summit, and the second encounter is another 10 minutes after that.

4. At the first of the two crossings, a sign notes there is 1.6 km remaining in your hike. You have travelled 1.4 km so far. The trail dips into a clump of forest on the other side of the road and then crosses a charming little wooden bridge.

5. On sunny, hot days, welcome shade is found as the trail meanders in and out of small islands of trees. With a sign marking 1.1 km to go, you cross Cosens Bay Rd. the second time. The patches of forest are left behind as you break out into another field of wild grasses.

6. Ten minutes later, at the far end of this meadow, trees blot the view of the lake once more. However, when this brief interruption is over, an expansive view of

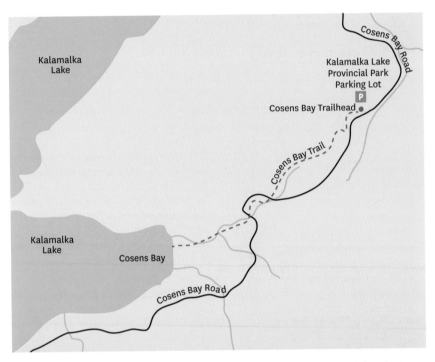

the lake greets you. A 10- to 15-minute drop delivers you to the sandy shoreline of Cosens Bay.

7. This is a magnificent place to swim, sit, think or just play in the sand. Amenities include picnic tables and an outhouse.

TOP: *The Cosens Bay trail provides little shelter from the summer sun, as this once green meadow can attest.*

BOTTOM: *Tranquil Cosens Bay and its warm summer waters are only a 3 km hike from Kalamalka Provincial Park parking area.*

OPPOSITE: *Cosens Bay seen from its beach extends outward to join Kalamalka Lake.*

5 Cougar Canyon

This hike provides spectacular views from a precarious perch, and some amazing exploration through a high-walled canyon.

CATEGORY: Return

DISTANCE: A: from Kalamalka Provincial Park parking lot – 14 km round trip; **B:** from Cougar Canyon hiking area parking lot – 5.5 km round trip (distance and time will depend on how much you explore the canyon floor)

HEIGHT GAIN: 172 m

HIGH POINT: 651 m

TIME: A: from Kalamalka Provincial Park parking lot – 4 hrs. round trip; **B:** from Cougar Canyon hiking area parking lot – 80 min. round trip

DIFFICULTY: Moderate

SEASONS: Late spring, summer, fall

TRAILHEAD COORDINATES: N50 12 34.2 W119 13 56.2

DIRECTIONS TO TRAILHEAD: In Vernon, at the major intersection of Highway 97 (32nd St.) and 25th Ave., drive east following the signs for Kalamalka Lake, Lumby, Nelson and Highway 6 South. Turn right onto Highway 6 and drive for less than a kilometre, looking for Kalamalka Lake Rd. Turn right onto Kalamalka Lake Rd. and stay on it for a little over 6 km before turning right onto Coldstream Creek Rd. Within 800 m, turn left onto Cosens Bay Rd. The parking lot is another 800 m down the road. Alternatively, follow Provincial Park signs directing you to Cosens Bay, starting at the intersection of Highway 6 and Kalamalka Lake Rd. through to the parking lot.

There are a couple of ways to arrive at this destination, and both are fantastic depending on your available time, the weather and, perhaps more importantly, your mood. The long version will take approximately two hours each way, while the short route will cost you substantially less time – about 80 minutes each way. I have provided both descriptions. The long route, call it A, simply starts at the Kalamalka Lake parking lot, while the short version, B, begins 4 km closer.

A:

1. At the Kalamalka Lake parking lot, look around for the large sign for the High Rim Trail (HRT). Much of the lower section of the trail includes the HRT. Beyond the sign, follow the narrow, single-track path along a barbed-wire fence on your left through an open, grassy hillside. Within a few minutes the trail brings you to a gate marked with a large NO TRESPASSING sign. Continue alongside the fence for a few more minutes until the path leaves the fenceline and begins its descent into the Beaver Valley. The edge of this drop forms the 1 km mark of the hike.

2. Continue the trek, following the well-placed HRT signage. The trail levels off in the valley bottom at the 1.2 km mark, where a sign steers you to the right. After the blazing sun, a gorgeously thick forest is a welcome change in this region of open meadows.

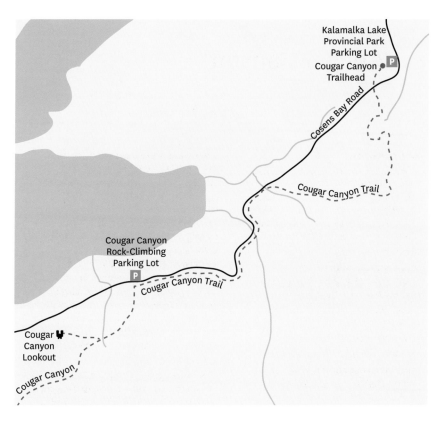

Kalamalka Lake
Provincial Park
Parking Lot

Cougar Canyon
Trailhead

Cosens Bay Road

Cougar Canyon Trail

Cougar Canyon
Rock-Climbing
Parking Lot

Cougar Canyon Trail

Cougar
Canyon
Lookout

Cougar Canyon

3. A few trails intersect the main trail you're on, but continue straight. At the 2.4 km point, the trail, and this beautiful Okanagan forest, deposits you onto Co-sens Bay Rd. This intersection is the lowest point of your journey, at 474 m, while the precarious perch you are hiking toward sits at 646 m – a gain of 172 m.

4. Turn left and hike up the road for 2 km while enjoying views of the shimmering blue-green water offered by Kalamalka Lake below you on your right. About 1 km up the road, power lines pass overhead and the road soon levels off.

5. Continue following the gravel road until you approach the marker on the left that indicates 4 km of road from the parking lot. Just beyond this, both trail and road cross underneath the power lines once again. On a rusted section on one of the power poles, the words COUGAR CANYON HIKING are clearly marked with white paint. An equally noticeable white arrow directs you to the left, into a forest.

6. Just beyond this marked pole there is an-other parking lot that is mainly used by rock climbers, as Cougar Canyon has some of the best rock walls in the Okanagan Valley. This parking lot is the beginning of the second, much shorter route into the canyon area.

B:

1. This second trail begins as an old forestry road and heads off into a forest. Five to ten minutes from the parking lot, the old for-estry road enters a wide clearing with an information kiosk at the far end. This kiosk is used by rock climbers and is supplied

TOP: *One of many magnificent rock outcroppings dominating the walls of Cougar Canyon.*

BOTTOM: *The blue-green waters of Kalamalka Lake seen from the Cougar Canyon viewpoint.*

OPPOSITE: *I met some friendly rock climbers while exploring Cougar Canyon. I sat for a while and chatted with them while we watched this fellow skilfully climb to the summit of this rock wall. They were a close-knit group: one couple had met while climbing these same rocks and soon got married.*

with maps of climbing routes as well as a chalkboard for noting route conditions. A sign attached to the kiosk warns against dropping rocks or debris over the edge of cliffs onto unsuspecting climbers.

2. The road has now been transformed into a narrow path that begins to climb and continues upward for about 10 minutes. When the trail plateaus, an abundance of signs once again warn about the hazards of tossing rocks over the edge of the cliffs. On your right a well-positioned park bench beckons your weary body. Take a seat and enjoy the spectacular view of Kalamalka Lake; there's no rush to get anywhere up here.

3. A few minutes beyond the bench, you will reach an important signed intersection. Going to the right will transport you to one of the best viewpoints in the region, while taking the left fork will drop you down into one of the most unique rock formations in the area. This is one of those rare occasions when you take both forks in a path.

4. The viewpoint is only five minutes away and the canyon floor is just twice that distance, so go and enjoy the viewpoint first, because you may not feel like it after you crawl up out of the canyon.

5. Once on the canyon floor, only minimal exploration is possible, as the trail seems to trickle to a stop once it passes the climbing areas. There is only one way to go, as the canyon is walled and narrow, but this is precisely the allure of this canyon. The steep walls and the rock formations kept me down there for the better part of an hour, just looking around and exploring the uniqueness of the landscape. I even met some friendly rock climbers who appeared to have enjoyed their day as much as I did.

6. Return the same way you came.

6 Ravine Edge

As the title suggests, this trek follows the lengthy edge of a ravine, presenting vistas of Kalamalka Lake and Lavington Valley. The end of the trail offers many options for exploring.

CATEGORY: Return

DISTANCE: 7 km round trip or up to 9 km, depending on your amount of exploring at the end of the trail

HEIGHT GAIN: 170 m
Elevation lost in the continuous descent from trailhead to destination is regained on the way back.

HIGH POINT: 1297 m

TIME: 2–3 hrs. round trip

DIFFICULTY: Moderately strenuous

SEASONS: Late spring, summer, fall

TRAILHEAD COORDINATES: N50 10 22.9 W119 12 09.1

DIRECTIONS TO TRAILHEAD: In Vernon, at the major intersection of Highway 97 (32nd St.) and 25th Ave., drive eastward, following the signs for Kalamalka Lake, Lumby, Nelson and Highway 6 South. Turn right onto Highway 6 and travel 8.8 km to King Edward Lake Forest Service Rd. on the right (south) side of the highway. This gravel road was unmarked at the time of writing, so pay attention to your odometer.

Reset your odometer to zero after turning onto King Edward Lake Forest Service Rd., because there are a few junctions to navigate, the first one being at the 4 km mark. Stay on the right-hand road here and continue driving to a junction at the 8.4 km mark. Take the right-hand road here as well. At 8.8 km, take the right-hand road once more. About 500 m later, this road crosses a small creek and you should see the trailhead sign on the right. Drive another 500 m to a large parking area and walk back to the trailhead.

1. This trail starts out briefly as a narrow, single-track path that parallels the left side of a fence made of horizontal fenceposts. It then heads to the left, away from the fence, into a thick, wondrous forest dotted with small clearings. Some of these clearings are decorated with the occasional birch and alder.

2. The trail is easy to follow, as an abundance of green arrows leave little doubt of where it travels. Less than a kilometre into the hike, the trail's namesake begins to take form as it approaches the edge of a ravine. This is the first of many viewpoints on this trek.

3. The trail traverses a large cutblock as it follows the ridgeline. A few feeder paths are picked up along the main trail, so keep your eye on the green arrow markers to ensure the correct route. The trail then descends steeply but briefly a couple of times as it ventures away from and then back to the ravine's edge.

4. About 2 km, or 30 to 35 minutes, into this hike, there is a significant unmarked junction. The trail is inland from the edge, travelling toward it, with a cutblock on the left. A well-trodden path approaches from the cutblock to join the main trail. This side trail

TOP: *The final ridge of Ravine Edge. From here there are several directions to roam free and explore various viewpoints.*

BOTTOM: *Lavington Valley, in the distance, is one of many spectacular sights along the Ravine Edge trek.*

Ravine Edge
Viewing

Ravine Edge
Viewing

Ravine
Edge
Parking
Lot P

Ravine
Edge
Trailhead

appears to be more travelled than the one you are currently on, but stay straight and follow the trail as it drops down through a thick forest. There is substantial overgrowth crossing the narrow trail, but this only lasts a couple of minutes.

5. Very soon the path makes a sharp 90° left turn after it has wrapped around the right side of a large-diameter conifer.

6. You should now be at the edge of a very steep ravine.

7. Follow the undulating trail as it accompanies the ridge on your right. Gradually it makes its way downward. You will see a boulder field quite a distance below you off your right shoulder. The trail descends farther downward on steep switchbacks through a dank forest, eventually reaching the massive rock field. This drop to the boulder field should take about 10 minutes.

8. A few minutes beyond the rubble, the trail meets the ravine once again. The path follows the edge of the ravine, taking a couple of different turns. Arrows mark the way to the northernmost edge, but for the most part it is hiker's choice. There is an incredible surplus of viewing attainable by finding different vantage points at the edge, so have fun exploring. In particular, Lavington Valley, the village of Coldstream and Kalamalka Lake are the highlights.

7 Enderby Cliffs

This is a favourite climb for locals as well as tourists. Its summit is one of the highest and most easily accessible ridges in the North Okanagan, and though it is a challenge, the scenery is worth the effort.

CATEGORY: Return

DISTANCE: 13 km round trip

HEIGHT GAIN: 721 m

HIGH POINT: 1184 m

TIME: 3.5–5 hrs. round trip

DIFFICULTY: Strenuous

SEASONS: Summer, fall

TRAILHEAD COORDINATES: N50 34 32.2 W119 06 16.6

DIRECTIONS TO TRAILHEAD: From Vernon, travel north on Highway 97A for about 36 km to the village of Enderby. In the middle of town, turn right onto Cliff Rd. and drive 2 km to Brash Allen Rd. Within 1.4 km the road turns to gravel, but the parking lot is just another 1.5 km down Brash Allen Rd. From the highway the route is clearly marked all the way with blue Provincial Park signs directing you to Enderby Cliffs Protected Area.

1. The trail is easily picked up kitty-corner to the parking lot. It begins as a dirt path that parallels a fence on the left and a gravel road on the right. A couple of minutes up the trail, you will need to make your way through a wooden entrance gate. A sign here informs you that there are lookouts at the 2 km and 3 km points along the trail, but up this path, named Tplaqin Trail, these lookouts are not marked. The sign also notifies you that the distance to the summit is 7 km.

2. The way is easy from here, as there really isn't any other place to go; this is the only trail you will come across on this hike.

3. The route is a steady skyward ascent that is quite gradual. Overall, the elevation gain is accomplished with a combination of flats, dips and rises, so there aren't any straight-up heart-pounding stretches.

4. About a half-hour (2 km) into the hike, a barrier with a sign prohibiting travel on the main trail confronts you. This is the first of many such barriers and signs along the trail. The alternative routes are obvious, and in this case there is a diversion that drops down to the right. The major monument at this juncture is a large crucifix that was carved by the villagers of Oberammergau, Germany.

5. For another half-hour or so the forest becomes increasingly deciduous. It is a subtle change, but as the path progresses, the forest changes, only to eventually be reclaimed by the darkness of cedars and hemlocks.

6. At the 3 km mark an amazing lookout point is evident as the trail opens up to a rock outcropping where the forest is behind you. Here, you have achieved 324 of the 721 m in height gain.

7. A good half-hour from the lookout, the path rounds a corner turning left that perches you on top of a wide, thinned forest that is sparse enough to tolerate substantial grassy undergrowth. Although the trail continues to gain moderate elevation, it is negligible compared to what you have accomplished to this point.

8. The path makes its way through the uncluttered trees for 5 to 10 minutes before approaching a superb lookout. This rocky

LEFT: *A unique view of the Salmon River Valley from the Enderby Cliffs.* COPYRIGHT BENLARHOME

BELOW: *Another sensational sight: looking south down the Salmon River Valley from Enderby Cliffs.* COPYRIGHT BENLARHOME

OPPOSITE: *Magnificent Enderby Cliffs seen from a rocky outcropping.* PHOTO: BRUCE ROBERTS–WARMHEARTMEDIA

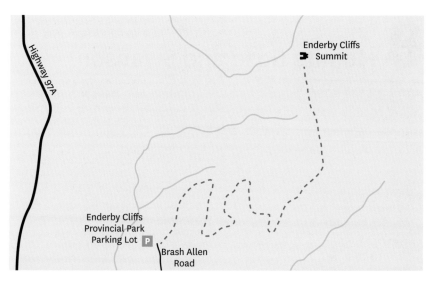

Enderby Cliffs
Summit

Highway 97A

Enderby Cliffs
Provincial Park
Parking Lot P

Brash Allen
Road

outcropping offers spectacular north and south panoramas of Pleasant Valley.

9. Beyond this lookout the grade gradually rises, making the 20- to 30-minute exertion to the summit a well-earned prize.

10. The landscapes from the viewpoint are wide and varied. Mountains, rivers, valleys, farmland and small villages are all in sight.

8 Mounts Rose and Swanson

Although the name suggests you will summit two peaks, that is certainly not the case. This is more of an extraordinary ridge walk that extends between Mounts Rose and Swanson. The panoramas are absolutely stunning, making the effort seemingly easy.

CATEGORY: Loop

DISTANCE: 7.2 km

HEIGHT GAIN: 245 m

HIGH POINT: 920 m

TIME: 2–3 hrs.

DIFFICULTY: Moderately strenuous

SEASONS: Late spring, summer, fall

TRAILHEAD COORDINATES: N50 27 42.6
 W119 16 06.1

DIRECTIONS TO TRAILHEAD: From Vernon drive north for about 23 km on Highway 97 to the village of Armstrong. As you enter the outskirts of the village, turn left onto Rosedale Ave. Drive down Rosedale for approximately 1.6 km to where it intersects with Pleasant Valley Rd. Turn right onto Pleasant Valley Rd. and continue along it for a little over a kilometre. At Bridge St., turn left, and because Bridge St. is short you will almost immediately turn left onto Wood Ave. Stay on Wood for about 1.5 km, and where it makes a sharp right turn it becomes Salmon River Rd. Salmon River Rd. soon makes a sharp 90° left turn, followed by a sharp right. About 1 km from the sharp right, you will meet Hallum Rd. on the left. Turn left onto Hallum and drive about 2 km to Chamberlain Rd. Turn left onto Chamberlain and follow it for roughly 1.75 km. When you come to a fork where Chamberlain Rd. continues to the right, take the left fork to find the trailhead parking lot 500 m farther along, on the left side of the road. The trailhead is at the far (west) end of the parking lot. There is another trail at the near end of the lot, but this is the exit of the loop and it is where you finish the trek. The trail is an old gravel road that begins to climb immediately. Take note of the detailed signboard illustrating the trail grid.

1. The road climbs steadily, with only a couple of level breaks, for 2 km, which should take about half an hour.

2. The road will plateau at this point as it comes to the first of a few junctions. Both the left and right branches are clearly marked here: left for Mount Rose, right for Mount Swanson. Both of these designations are slightly misleading, however, since the trail to Mount Rose actually

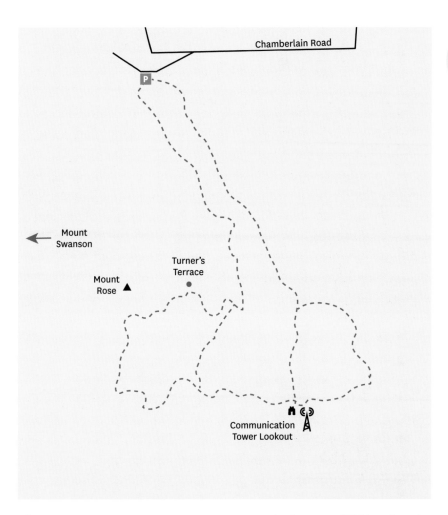

takes you to a communication tower on the southwest flank of Mount Rose, while the Mount Swanson choice leads slightly to the west of Mount Rose. The entire route can be somewhat confusing, but if you do not concern yourself with where you are, and simply follow the trails, you will enjoy an incredible journey with magnificent views.

3. So, turn right following the Mount Swanson sign and walk this wonderful 2.5 km loop that hooks up with the Mount Rose trail, taking you to the same communication tower. Within a few minutes, you will arrive at a terrace marked as "Turner's Terrace." As the trail progresses, the sights become increasingly spectacular. The trail undulates, dipping into a couple of small valleys. At about 1.6 km from the Mounts Swanson and Rose intersection, you will come across a lesser trail going to the left. Stay straight and carry on to the tower about 800 to 900 m farther.

4. There may not be a better view of Pleasant Valley anywhere than from this tower lookout. Otter Lake is the first visible body

of water, and beyond that is Swan Lake on the left and Okanagan Lake on the right.

5. Return to the trail and walk past the tower to find a narrow single-track trail that heads into the forest. Enjoy the scenery up top, because although the remaining 2.5 km downhill walk in the woods is very pleasant, it leaves all of the best sights behind.

TOP: *A sensational panorama of the fertile farmland of Pleasant Valley as seen from Mount Rose.*

BOTTOM: *This communication tower on the southwest flank of Mount Rose is a great spot for surveying Pleasant Valley.*

OPPOSITE, TOP: *Much of the Mounts Rose and Swanson day hike takes you through gorgeous, dense, coniferous forests.*

OPPOSITE, BOTTOM: *Several aged signs on this tree provide very little in the way of accurate directions, but they do add character to the hike.*

9 Grey Canal Trail

*The Grey Canal system was engineered to supply the benchlands sur-
rounding Vernon with much-needed water at these high elevations.
Although water was plentiful in the lower districts, the benchlands
were dry for much of the growing season, and if fruit farming was to
flourish here, it would need a continuous flow of precious water.*

*The massive project was begun in 1905, and $423,000 later it was
completed in 1914. Not only was the endless supply of water from high-
land lakes used for fruit farming, there was demand from ranchers as
well. The highly successful canal was used until it was shut down in
1970 as more modern methods of irrigation came into use.*

*The canal trail is segmented, as only portions of it have been re-
tained as hiking/biking trails. The section detailed in this chapter is a
10 km partial loop, with the trailhead at the northernmost point of the
Grey Canal Trail system at Glenhayes Rd. It crosses McLennan Rd. and
Rugg Rd. along its path.*

*Even though this section of trail is within city limits, I chose this portion
because it is more removed from the city, though the farther south the
trail goes, the denser the urbanization becomes. An additional factor
with this choice of trail section is that it simply presents the most magnificent views of Swan Lake, Pleasant Valley and the city of Vernon. As
the trail approaches newly developed subdivisions, its dependence on
paved roads intensifies and the views diminish as the elevation drops.*

CATEGORY: Return, with a loop at the far
end

DISTANCE: 10 km round trip

HEIGHT GAIN: Nominal

HIGH POINT: 584 m

TIME: 2.5–3 hrs. round trip

DIFFICULTY: Moderate

SEASONS: Early spring, summer, late fall

TRAILHEAD COORDINATES: N50 20 16.5
W119 13 49.9

DIRECTIONS TO TRAILHEAD: Travelling
north from Vernon on Highway 97, turn
right onto Elmwood Rd. At a T-junction at
the top of Elmwood Rd. (about 200 m),
turn right onto Pleasant Valley Rd. and
then immediately take a wide left turn to
get onto L & A Rd. Drive along L & A Rd.
for about 1 km to where it becomes Baker–
Hogg Rd. Continue along Baker–Hogg for
800 m and turn right on Glenhayes Rd. The
parking lot is marked on the left side of the
road, 600 m up Glenhayes Rd.

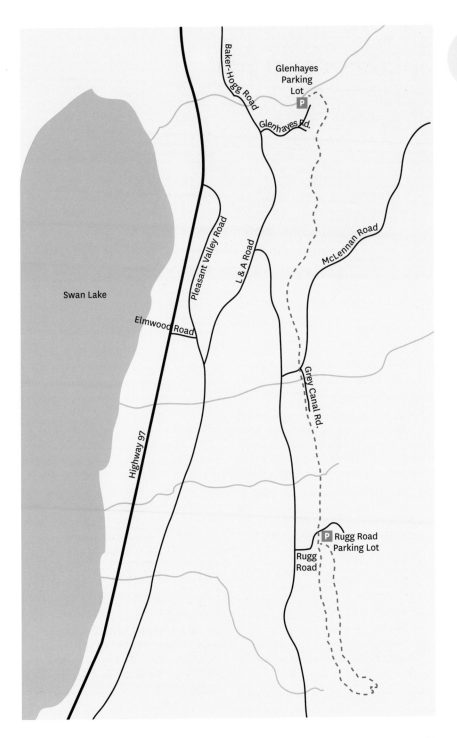

1. After parking, you'll see a sign directing you to walk 100 m up the road to the trailhead on the right.

2. Pass through a narrow gate and immediately drop into the V-shaped canal, emerging after a few minutes to parallel the canal on your left. Suddenly the view opens up.

3. As you look to the west, Swan Lake and the Bella Vista Hills dominate the landscape. Views of Pleasant Valley can be observed to the north and they become even more sprawling as you travel farther south.

4. As the path travels beside the canal, it dodges in and out of small pockets of forest that probably have sprouted directly from the effects of the canal's payload over the years.

5. With over a kilometre gained, the first signs of the canal's remains become evident. Wooden trestles, cement foundations, concrete transfer stations and galvanized troughs litter the landscape. It is beautiful to see what is left of this wondrous man-made creation. Interpretive signs are appropriately placed along the pathway.

6. Forty minutes into the trek, the path navigates another narrow gate and crosses McLennan Rd. to emerge onto Grey Canal Rd. Stay on this paved road for about 10 minutes to the end of the road.

7. The route gets back onto the trail after it passes through another narrow gate. You will notice there is progressively more development as you cover more ground walking south.

8. Some 3.5 km from the trailhead, you come to the Rugg Rd. access. This large gravel parking lot has two trails leaving it, one on either side. The trail on the left goes steeply upward, higher into the hills, while the lower one, to the right, sticks to the canal. Good news: take the low trail on the right.

9. Roughly 1.5 km of drifting on this scenic trail brings you to a prominent junction. Taking the right fork would bring you to the intersection of Silver Star Rd. and Blackcomb Way. Take the left route instead and briefly climb uphill to a parking lot.

10. The trail leaves the parking lot from the far side. This trail loops back to the Rugg Rd. parking lot, closing a loop as it rejoins the parking lot. This is the same trail that exits the left side of the Rugg Rd. parking lot going steeply uphill.

11. After a little over a kilometre, this flat upper trail briefly drops, bringing you back to the Rugg Rd. parking lot.

12. From here, return to the Glenhayes Rd. parking lot on the same route that brought you here.

TOP: *The hillside stroll on the Grey Canal trail offers panoramic sights of Swan Lake, the city of Vernon and the benchlands on the opposite (west) side of Swan Lake.*

BOTTOM: *Swan Lake is one of the many standout features of the Grey Canal hike.*

OPPOSITE: *A section of deciduous forest on the Grey Canal Trail.*

10 Oyama Lookout

This journey incorporates portions of the High Rim Trail (HRT) to reach its final destination, so the trail is well marked with a combination of HRT signs and green arrows supplied by the Vernon Outdoors Club. The summit shows off a splendid view of Vernon and Kalamalka Lake, though the view is shared with a communication tower.

CATEGORY: Return

DISTANCE: 8.4 km round trip

HEIGHT GAIN: 160 m

HIGH POINT: 1455 m

TIME: 2.5–3 hrs. round trip

DIFFICULTY: Moderately strenuous

SEASONS: Late spring, summer, fall

TRAILHEAD COORDINATES: N50 07 43.6 W119 17 38.8

DIRECTIONS TO TRAILHEAD: From Vernon, drive roughly 16 km south on Highway 97 to Oyama. Turn left on Oyama Rd. as it splits the waters of Wood and Kalamalka lakes. Drive for 1.7 km to Middle Bench Rd. Turn right on Middle Bench. Almost immediately, turn left onto Todd Rd. Less than a kilometre up Todd Rd., turn right onto Oyama Lake Rd. Signs to Oyama Lake Resort will have directed you this far as well.

Oyama Lake Rd. instantly becomes a gravel road. Drive 9.2 km on the gravel and turn left. The route to Oyama Lake Resort continues to the right. One kilometre farther on, take another left, and about 400 m up the road you'll see a parking area in a grassy pullout.

1. The path begins as a wide, grassed-over, inactive logging road. Eventually the level trail narrows and within 10 minutes the first green arrow sends you to the right. Glance down below you on the right side of the trail to see the marshy water system called Chatterton Lake. At this point, look for a multi-directional sign posted on a tree confirming that the Oyama lookout is 2.7 km up the trail. There really hasn't been much elevation gain yet, and other than a few insignificant ripples on the trail, the path remains level for quite a while.

2. A few more green arrows keep you on the path while you stroll through this peaceful forest. A pattern of weaving and rolling up and down through small shallow gullies becomes repetitive. About 3 km (40–45 minutes) from the trailhead, however, the route widens to a grass road once again. Almost five minutes later, you will notice the first of two grassed-over roads approaching from the left.

3. The first road is unmarked, but the second one, a few minutes on, has a marker on a tree pointing the way to Damer Lake. Turn left and head up this road. Although at the time of writing there was not a marker indicating that Oyama Lookout is up this road, it certainly is. From this junction you can see a noteworthy gravel road just ahead – if you end up on this, you have gone too far.

4. Now, about 15–20 m up the road you just turned onto, a green sign, low to the ground, steers you off the road, to the right and into the bush. As you approach this sign, bend over and take a close look at it, because it has a handwritten message that says 5 M FARTHER. So, go 5 m farther and take the trail upward into the bush.

This very brief diversion plants you onto another inactive dirt and grass road. Turn left and the road follows a power line that supplies the tower at the summit of Oyama Lookout. A few minutes up this road, take note of signage for Damer Lake lookout, on the right.

5. Around the 4 km mark, or one hour into the hike, the trail passes under the power line as it enters a large clearing. At the far end of the clearing, make your way to another green arrow marker, which will send you down a road that exits the left end of the clearing. The power line is off to your left.

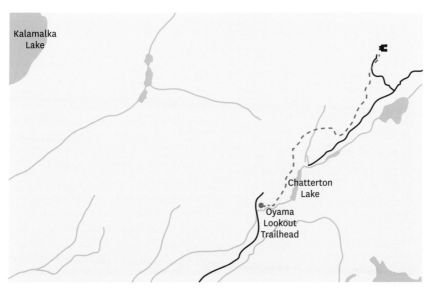

From the Oyama Lookout trail. As greater elevation is gained, outlying hills and forests become a more common sight.

6. Within five minutes the trail opens to another clearing and the power line joins the journey again. Once more a green arrow at the far end of the clearing sends you to the left. This time, you are departing the main road as you begin to climb. The tower comes into view.

7. The balance of the journey is an uphill section that will take about 10–15 minutes, depending on your level of fitness. Near the end of the trek, the trail crosses a service road. You either sprint or gasp your way to the summit. Your choice.

8. The view from the top is stunning.

TOP: *Vernon and Kalamalka Lake from Oyama Lookout.*

BOTTOM: *Damer Lake is nestled just a short distance off the Oyama Lookout trail.*

11 Rimrocks

This quick stroll provides a bounty of rewards including a lava bed, lava spires, tremendous views of Coldstream and Vernon Hill, an abandoned panel truck, and a good workout for the heart. All this within a 45-minute trek one way.

CATEGORY: Return

DISTANCE: 6 km round trip

HEIGHT GAIN: 177 m

HIGH POINT: 1160 m

TIME: 1.5–2 hrs. round trip

DIFFICULTY: Moderate

SEASONS: Late spring, summer, fall

TRAILHEAD COORDINATES: N50 11 27.3 W119 09 24.4

DIRECTIONS TO TRAILHEAD: In Vernon, at the major intersection of Highway 97 (32nd St.) and 25th Ave., drive east, following the signs for Kalamalka Lake, Lumby, Nelson and Highway 6 South. Turn right onto Highway 6 and travel 8.8 km to King Edward Lake Forest Service Rd. on the right (south) side of the highway. This gravel road was unmarked at the time of writing, so pay attention to your odometer. At 3.9 km, stay straight, leaving King Edward Lake Forest Service Rd., which veers off to the right. At 5.5 km from the highway, a hike sign is easily seen on the right side of the road. Park on the left side of the road.

1. The trailhead begins to the immediate right of a barbed-wire fence. Don't take the trail on the inside of the fence. Right away the trail becomes a double-wide former forestry road progressing steadily uphill. Although this region is classified as semi-arid, there are surprisingly dense forests such as this one, consisting of thick-trunked hemlock and western red cedar.

2. Twenty minutes into the hike, with the first kilometre behind you, the path makes a steep ascent, and five minutes into this climb you'll see an abandoned panel truck sitting quietly off to the right side of the trail – an exploration gone bad or a joy ride gone well? Either way, it would have been a long walk back to town. You'll cross a barbed-wire fence through a gate here. Be sure to close the gate, as cattle graze in this area.

3. Immediately beyond the fence, look for a couple of green arrow markers in quick succession that will send you to the left at a minor junction and then left again. At the other end of these two markers the forest opens up, plateaus and begins to deteriorate, gradually becoming a single-track path.

4. Spectacular vistas of the East Vernon townships of Lavington and Coldstream and hills across the Coldstream Valley begin to present themselves. At about the 2 km mark, the trek reaches its maximum elevation as well as its maximum viewing. You will pop in and out of a sparse forest as you safely parallel a cliff's edge for about 1 km until the trail's end is reached.

5. The destination is unlike anything else in the vicinity. Massive lava beds, thousands of years old, are stretched out beneath you, a hundred metres below. Erosion has left spires standing 15–20 metres high. This is a barren landscape that appears devoid of life. It is an absolute treasure.

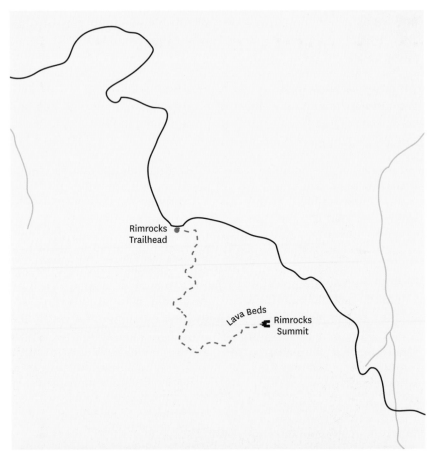

Rimrocks
Trailhead

Lava Beds Rimrocks
Summit

TOP: *This abandoned panel truck has seen better days and is now an established landmark on the Rimrocks trail.*

BOTTOM: *From the Rimrocks ridge looking due north presents views of the Coldstream Valley.*

OPPOSITE: *The main attraction of the Rimrocks trail is the magnificent lava spires.*

12 Shorts Creek Canyon Rim

A spectacular hike that provides views of Shorts Creek Canyon, Terrace Mountain and Okanagan Lake. Most of the moderate elevation gain is felt near the end of the expedition.

CATEGORY: Return

DISTANCE: 9.8 km round trip to the true summit

HEIGHT GAIN: 226 m

HIGH POINT: 1548 m

TIME: 3–4 hrs.

DIFFICULTY: Moderately strenuous

SEASONS: Late spring, summer, early fall

TRAILHEAD COORDINATES: N50 09 38.0 W119 34 54.2

DIRECTIONS TO TRAILHEAD: From Vernon, drive north on Highway 97, and at the north end of Swan Lake continue on Highway 97, following the signs for Kamloops. Travel 5.6 km, driving past the Spallumcheen golf course and Historic O'Keefe Ranch, and highway signs will direct you down Westside Rd. toward Fintry and Killiney. Continue along Westside Rd. for 18 km to Beau Park Rd. on your right.

Reset your odometer; there are kilometre markers along this gravel road, but do not confuse them with the distances you will travel to arrive at the destination. The course is obvious, but there are a few turns that will require minor detailed descriptions.

At the 2.5 km point, stay left, leaving Beau Park Rd. and joining Bouleau Lake Rd. At 4.6 and 7.6 km, veer left again, now joining Whiteman Creek Rd. Veer left again at 8.3 km. Turn left at 9.9 km, leaving the main branch of Whiteman Creek Rd., immediately crossing a short bridge. A green arrow pointing to the left is another indicator of where this left diversion must be made. The gravel road begins to climb.

At 15.5 km, make sure you follow the road on the right. There is an arrow marker here as well. Then, 200 m on, take the left fork, where a HIKING TRAIL sign is posted. At 16.9 km, stay to your left, and another 500 m farther will bring you to the trailhead, where there is an old logging landing to park on.

1. The trail begins as a wide, exposed path lined with beautiful alders. While it appears that the trail persists on this wide path, it does not. Within 4–5 minutes, the trail to the canyon rim juts off to the left as a narrow path through the trees. This is marked by an unmistakable green arrow on a tree, as well as an old plank sign saying TRAIL with an arrow pointing to the left. Hard to miss.

2. The now single-track path gently undulates as it follows a slope.

3. After the first kilometre (15 minutes), the path comes close to the canyon edge, and the cliffs of the other side of the canyon become visible. These cliffs are your ultimate destination.

4. Five minutes later the trail drops slightly to cross one of the narrow tributaries of Attenborough Creek. Then two more small creeks are crossed in succession within 5–7 minutes.

5. Half an hour, or about 2 km, into the hike the trail presents magnificent, though brief, views down the canyon.

6. For the next 20 minutes, the trail alternates between steep climbs and plateaus until it presents a stunning viewpoint. You have hiked approximately 3 km.

7. For almost 2 km beyond this, the path climbs off and on as it delivers occasional panoramas of the canyon and surrounding mountains, but nothing is as fulfilling as reaching the impressive summit of the canyon rim.

8. There are a couple of false summits as you climb, and even when the maximum elevation is gained, there is still more to see with another 10 minutes of level walking

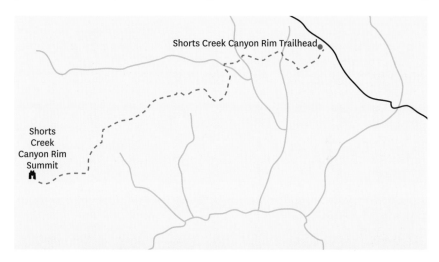

This section of the Shorts Creek Canyon Rim trail is a pleasant stroll through an open coniferous forest.

TOP: *Shorts Creek canyon viewed from the Shorts Creek Canyon Rim trail.*

BOTTOM: *Shorts Creek canyon seen from a higher vantage point along the Shorts Creek Canyon Rim trail.*

OPPOSITE, TOP: *Terrace Mountain stands out as an unmistakable landmark on the Shorts Creek Canyon Rim trek.*

OPPOSITE, BOTTOM: *Okanagan Lake in the distance from the summit of Shorts Creek Canyon Rim.*

beyond the summit. This additional 10 minutes provides tremendous rewards.

9. Terrace Mountain is the standout, 5.6 km due south. Glimpses of Okanagan Lake can be seen to the southeast (left) and Shorts Creek Canyon is directly beneath you. Making this trek gifts you with an immense day. This is truly one of the best hikes in the North Okanagan.

13 Fintry Falls

This is a day of exploring and wonder, as this trip offers two out-standing adventures. As the name suggests, Fintry Falls is the main attraction, but a lengthy trail leaves the falls walk and meanders on a hillside slope providing spectacular views of Okanagan Lake and of Ellison Ridge across the lake. History is evident throughout the area and is certainly worth investigating. Captain James Cameron Dun-Waters was a wealthy young Scot who inherited a fortune at the age of 22. His love for travel and hunting brought him to Shorts Point in 1908, and within a year he purchased the land and renamed it "Fintry" after his Scotland home. Dun-Waters returned to Fintry after the First World War and created an extraordinary estate there. Many of the structures are still standing and several have been restored.

Fintry Falls viewing only, from top platform:

CATEGORY: Return

DISTANCE: 1.5 km round trip

HEIGHT GAIN: 87 m

HIGH POINT: 428 m

TIME: 20–30 min. round trip

DIFFICULTY: Easy

SEASONS: Spring, summer, fall

Fintry Falls top platform combined with hillside stroll:

CATEGORY: Return with some loops

DISTANCE: up to 5 km

HEIGHT GAIN: 87 m

HIGH POINT: 428 m

TIME: up to 1.5 hrs.

DIFFICULTY: Easy

SEASONS: Spring, summer, fall

TRAILHEAD COORDINATES: N50 08 17.1 W119 30 09.2

DIRECTIONS TO TRAILHEAD: From Vernon, drive north on Highway 97, and at the north end of Swan Lake continue on Highway 97, following the road signs for Kamloops. Travel 5.6 km, driving past the Spallumcheen golf course and Historic O'Keefe Ranch, and highway signs will direct you down Westside Rd. toward Fintry and Killiney. Drive south for about 34 km to Fintry Delta Rd. off the left side of Westside Rd. You are now entering Fintry Provincial Park. Travel 2.1 km to the parking lot on the left side of the road.

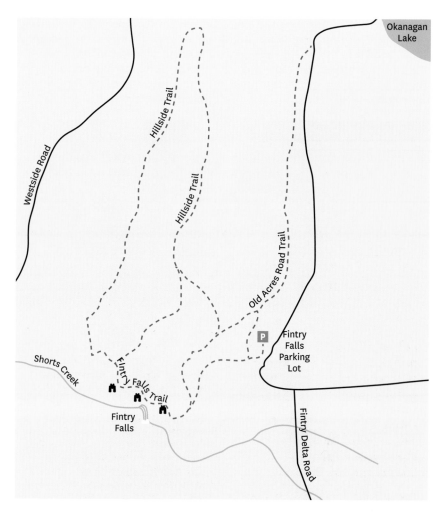

1. The falls are easy to find, as the trailhead exits the parking lot with adequate signage. Just follow the FINTRY FALLS signs and within a couple of minutes you will be greeted by approximately 400 wooden stairs. The views of the falls are accessed by this construction of beams, braces and steps in order to prevent human erosion of the canyon walls and of course keep people from falling into the canyon. There are three viewing platforms, evenly spaced to pace the climb. A total of 87 m is gained rather quickly. I urge you to go to the top platform for the rear view of the falls and for a spectacular panorama of Okanagan Lake and the ridges and hills above the lake's eastern shore.

2. Although this is a short hike, there is more to see and explore. On the way up the staircase, you will notice a gap in the railing on the right. This is an exit to the hills above the campground. There are a couple of routes to take, allowing for a leisurely walk on this hillside.

3. The main trail, called the Old Access Road Trail, loops back down to the parking lot. There is a short branch on the left side about 500 m along that allows you to venture higher up for even more magnificent viewing.

4. There are also access trails to the campground that will bypass the parking lot altogether, so pay attention to your exit strategy. There's much to see up here and the grade is relatively level once you have conquered that staircase.

ABOVE: *Fintry Falls from one of three viewing platforms.*

OPPOSITE, TOP: *A daunting sight. A portion of the steep stairway to the viewing platforms for Fintry Falls.*

OPPOSITE, BOTTOM: *A backside view of Fintry Falls from the uppermost platform.*

TOP: *Spectacular vistas of Okanagan Lake and the surrounding countryside can be seen from the rolling hillsides to the north of Fintry Falls.*

BOTTOM: *Many of the buildings of the Fintry Estate have been restored and can be explored by the public.*

14 Sugarloaf Mountain

CATEGORY: Return

DISTANCE: 5 km round trip

HEIGHT GAIN: 323 m

HIGH POINT: 1035 m

TIME: 1.5–2 hrs. round trip

DIFFICULTY: Moderately strenuous

SEASONS: Spring, summer, fall

TRAILHEAD COORDINATES: N50 12 52.5 W119 29 51.3

DIRECTIONS TO TRAILHEAD: From Vernon, drive north on Highway 97, and at the north end of Swan Lake continue on Highway 97, following the road signs for Kamloops. Travel for 5.6 km, driving past the Spallumcheen golf course and Historic O'Keefe Ranch, and highway signs will direct you down Westside Rd. toward Fintry and Killiney. Drive 23.2 km to North Westside Rd., turning right up this road. Even though there is not a proper street marker, you will know you are on the correct road when you spot a large wooden sign saying SUGARLOAF MOUNTAIN fastened to a large tree on your left at the start of the gravel road. You will also see a sign directing you to the 'North Westside Road Waste Transfer Station & Recycling Depot.' The road turns to gravel within 100 meters. Carry on upward for 3.75 km, looking for the green and white hiking trail sign on the left side of the road.

1. After a momentary uphill burst into a forest of spruce and pine, the trail comes to a fork as it is joined by another trail coming in from the left. However, with two arrow markers immediately guiding you to the right, the correct path is easily recognized. The other trail continues straight upward. Both trails ultimately join about 15 minutes later, but the path to the right is a much easier route.

2. Within another 300 m or so, you'll come to another junction. Again a marker will steer you in the correct direction (straight). From here the trail begins an upward climb, and as you ascend, a third sign sends you to the right. The trail becomes narrow and the grade decreases, even becoming level in spots.

3. Fifteen minutes into the hike, you will meet up with the trail you departed from at the start of the hike. This is the 1 km mark of the journey, and as you approach it the path plateaus at the crest of a rise. Here you catch the first glimpse of Okanagan Valley beauty, with a wonderful view of Whiteman Creek Valley.

4. You now come to a small clearing on a broad ledge. The trail resumes beyond some sizable rocks at the far end of this clearing.

5. Two more signs direct you to your left, this time just a few minutes up the path. Switchbacks become the dominant feature as you challenge your lung capacity for nearly 500 m. There are a couple of reprieves when the trail levels off periodically, but it then switches back and forth for an additional 500 m.

6. At the 2 km mark, the path flattens and the forest thickens for the final 10-minute strut to the viewpoint.

7. Be careful – the edge appears abruptly and the drop is sudden and lengthy. As much as this panorama of Okanagan Lake is spectacular, it is even more expansive if you venture a bit farther to the left (south) to the true viewpoint.

8. Remove your pack, sit down and take in this immense view of Okanagan Lake. Even on a dank, wet, cool autumn day, I was nevertheless enchanted by this spectacular view.

TOP: *Looking southward over Okanagan Lake from the summit of Sugarloaf Mountain. This sight is spectacular even on a gloomy day.*

BOTTOM: *Looking across Okanagan Lake from the summit of Sugarloaf Mountain.*

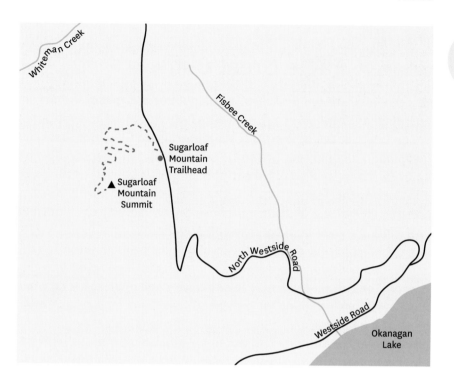

15 Eagle Crest Cliffs

This gem of a hike was bushwhacked, flagged and tagged by the owner-operators of the charming "Cozy Cabins Nature Resort" on Creighton Valley Rd. Over the past several years Harald and Kim Hatterscheidt have made a noble effort to mark nearby trails with proper signage and directions for the enjoyment of their guests as well as the local population. Their generosity, however, has been repaid with destruction and vandalism, as their signs have been removed from roadways and trails and their markers taken off of trees.

In an effort to provide superb scenic viewing for their guests' enjoyment, Harald set out across the road from his resort and developed his own trail on private land, also taking advantage of pre-existing trails and forest service roads on provincial park land as well as Crown land. The beauty of this combination of trails is that they are in an area where there is no active logging. Harald has created a masterpiece and I strongly urge you to take a few hours out of your day to enjoy the glorious viewing on rock bluffs that he worked so hard to share with you.

CATEGORY: Return

DISTANCE: 6 km round trip

HEIGHT GAIN: 325 m

HIGH POINT: 1176 m

TIME: 2.5–3 hrs.

DIFFICULTY: Moderately strenuous

SEASONS: Summer, fall

TRAILHEAD COORDINATES: N50 12 20.3 W118 43 48.8

DIRECTIONS TO TRAILHEAD: From the 4-way stop on Highway 6 in the gorgeous hamlet of Lumby, drive east for 1.7 km to Creighton Valley Rd. on the right (south) side of the highway. Travel Creighton Valley Rd. for 18.6 km to the Cozy Cabins Nature Resort on the right side of the road. Creighton Valley Rd. succumbs to gravel at the 7.4 km mark. Kim and Harald Hatterscheidt will graciously allow you to park your vehicle at their resort, but please ask their permission first. Alternatively, there is a parking pullout about 500 m down the road on the left.

1. The trailhead is easy to find. From the resort, walk down the road counting the power line poles until you reach the fourth one. The first pole counted is directly across the road from the resort. The trail is on the left and is marked with orange flagging. There is a 20 km marker on a tree on the opposite side of the road as well.

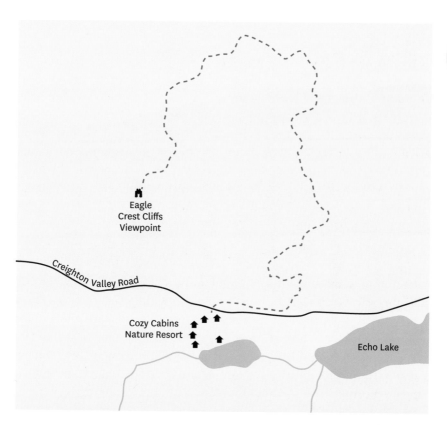

The climb to Eagle Crest Cliffs begins as an old, wide dirt road.

TOP: *Looking across Creighton Valley from Eagle Crest Cliffs.*

BOTTOM: *Watch your footing while exploring the Eagle Crest Cliffs. Many large boulders have separated, opening shallow chasms.*

OPPOSITE: *Echo Lake from Eagle Crest Cliffs.*

2. The trail through a forest of western red cedar and western hemlock begins as an old road, but it transforms into a single-track trail some 5–7 minutes later when another trail approaches from the left. Stay on the main trail going up to the right. The path from this fork turns into a gentle rise for a few minutes before becoming a steep climb.

3. Now, it appears that Harald is in better physical condition than I am, because he did not feel the need to include any switchbacks on this steep ascent, but instead took a straight-upward approach. This abrupt direct climb lasts for about 15–20 minutes. Enjoy!

4. The grade diminishes a few minutes after it meets and rises alongside an avalanche slope on the right of the trail. A few minutes after the trail begins to ease off, it intersects with an inactive logging road. This junction is unmistakable and will also be straightforward to find on the way back, as Harald has placed a large pile of boulders at this junction. You have now hiked just short of 2 km.

5. Turn left up the road and relish the reduced uphill rise. Just under 10 minutes of hiking up the road, another road approaches from the right. Stick to the left on the main thoroughfare. Roughly five minutes from this tributary, a fainter road goes off to the left. Take this left trail, leaving the main road. Harald has marked this trail very well with orange and blue ribbons, making it extremely difficult to miss.

6. Five minutes along this level track brings you to a small meadow, and once more, well-placed orange markers to your left will direct you out of the meadow and back into the forest.

7. Now walking on a slight downhill gradient, you reach the rock cliffs in about five minutes. Continue watching for markers to deliver you to the edge of the cliffs, all the while keeping an eye on your footing. There are sudden dropoffs, sinkholes and ankle-twisting rocks here. It should take an additional 5–10 minutes to reach the exceptional viewing on the edge of the cliffs.

8. Looking to the left (east), your eyes are drawn by the vast expanse of Echo Lake, while the view to the west includes both Barbe Lakes and a twisting Creighton Valley.

9. Return the same way.

16 Rawlings Lake Cliffs

Although some sources warn that portions of this route travel through private property, there are no signs to indicate this except for one asking you to close a gate behind you. Nonetheless, all trekking routes should be treated with a high standard of regard.

CATEGORY: Return

DISTANCE: 9.6 km round trip

HEIGHT GAIN: 454 m

HIGH POINT: 1023 m

TIME: 1.5–2 hrs. to the summit

DIFFICULTY: Strenuous

SEASONS: Summer, fall

TRAILHEAD COORDINATES: N50 16 00.6 W118 53 07.9

DIRECTIONS TO TRAILHEAD: From the four-way stop in Lumby, drive east on Highway 6 for 5 km to Rawlings Lake Rd. Turn left onto Rawlings Lake Rd. and drive 2 km to Brookfield Rd. on the left. Park anywhere on either road wherever it is safe to pull over. There is enough room to park on the right where Brookfield Rd. begins. From your parked vehicle on Brookfield, cross Rawlings Lake Rd. to get to the trailhead. The trail is unmarked and simply heads into a forest.

1. The route begins as a twin-track forest road, and within a couple of minutes the aforementioned gate needs to be crossed. And yes, please do close it behind you.

2. A few minutes past the gate, the trail opens to a rather large field the takes about a minute to cross before going back into the forest.

3. The trail begins to climb steeply, with the grade lessening from time to time for the next 15 minutes. During this preliminary uphill climb, the 1 km point of the hike occurs where the trail passes through a non-gated fence.

4. About five minutes beyond the fence, the trail levels off for a few minutes. This is the first of only a few plateaus as the path continues its skyward ascent for another 20 to 30 minutes.

5. A trail deviating off to the left to a magnificent viewpoint is easily noted at about the 2 km mark (35 to 40 minutes from the trailhead, or about 20 minutes from the fence).

6. Almost 3 km from the base of the trailhead, the path enters a large logged-off area. Still walking upward, wander on what has now become a skidder trail through this wide-open cutblock for about five minutes, finally intersecting with a key gravelled logging road as the skidder trail reaches its zenith.

7. Turn right onto this major road and saunter through the mayhem of fallen trees and debris for roughly 5 to 10 minutes. You need to pay close attention to the right side of the road while making your way up this logging road, as the old trail is found off this side. It's easy to see if you're looking for it. There are no trail markers anywhere along this entire system.

8. The final leg into the edge of the cliffs is an easy five-minute stroll through open forest. There are a couple of minor trails taking you to different vantage points.

9. The view across Creighton Valley is impressive, with the Camel's Hump being the most prominent feature in the distance, 13 km to the southeast.

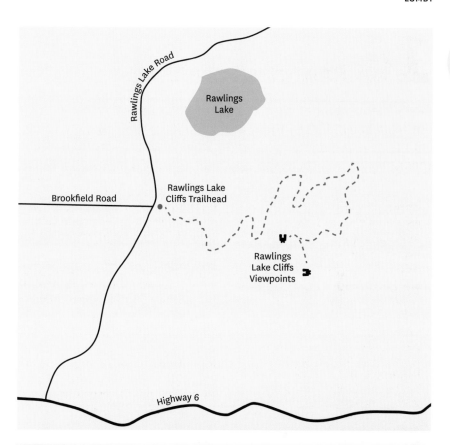

The going is easy here at the beginning of the Rawlings Lake Cliffs trail, but soon the route begins its relentless climb.

TOP: *Remnants of logging in a large clear-cut.*

BOTTOM: *Rawlings Lake Cliffs roadside view.*

OPPOSITE, TOP: *This astonishing panorama of the Creighton Valley is seen from the summit of Rawlings Lake Cliffs. The "Camel's Hump" is the knoll to the immediate left.*

OPPOSITE, BOTTOM: *Rawlings Lake from a trailside viewpoint.*

17 Denison Lake

This hike is a leisurely stroll through a gorgeous forest of spruce and birch, with a wonderfully quiet lake as a destination. Without motorized traffic accessing the lake, people and noise are scarce.

CATEGORY: Return with an optional loop

DISTANCE: 8 km round trip

HEIGHT GAIN: Nominal

HIGH POINT: 1588 m

TIME: 2–3 hrs. round trip

DIFFICULTY: Moderate

SEASONS: Summer, early fall

TRAILHEAD COORDINATES: N50 10 08.2 W118 43 33.5

The above values for distance, elevation change and time do not include an alternative return loop.

DIRECTIONS TO TRAILHEAD: From the four-way stop in the hamlet of Lumby, drive east on Highway 6 for 1.7 km to Creighton Valley Rd., on the right (south) side of the highway. Travel Creighton Valley Rd. for 15.8 km to meet up with Bonneau Forest Service Rd. on the right. Creighton Valley Rd. becomes gravel at the 7.4 km mark.

There are two parking options at the trailhead:

1) From the base of Bonneau FSR, drive 6.9 km to an unmarked grassy parking zone on the right side of the road. The trailhead makes its way into the forest on the right side of the parking area, and within a couple of short minutes the trail intersects with an inactive forestry road.

2) From the base of Bonneau FSR, drive 6.5 km to an inactive forestry road that shoots off from the right side of Bonneau FSR. This is the same road the above trail meets up with. This road stretches for more than 1 km before hitting an abrupt end, so some hiking distance can be reduced by driving up it. However, it becomes rougher as it progresses. A high-clearance vehicle is recommended.

This hike begins 800 m up the inactive forestry road at a cattle guard. I chose to stop at a pull-off here because I was driving my wife's vehicle, and travelling farther up the road could produce minor damage – likely scratches on her car – and we all know how that story would end.

1. The road becomes a single-track trail 10 minutes farther up, just past a minor parking lot.

2. Within a couple of minutes the trail crosses a narrow stream, the first of several crossings of the same stream within the next 10 minutes.

3. There is a narrow trail to the right roughly 2 km, or 30 minutes, into this trek. Take a quick look to see a massive boulder pile. There is an alternative return loop from the lake that exits at this junction. Come back and carry on up the main path.

4. The path begins to climb and continues upward, but only for five to six minutes before plateauing again.

5. Seven to eight minutes after levelling, the trail splits left and right. There is no signage, and both trails are marked with green arrows. Make sure you take the left fork. On your return, however, if you wish to take a longer, alternative route through

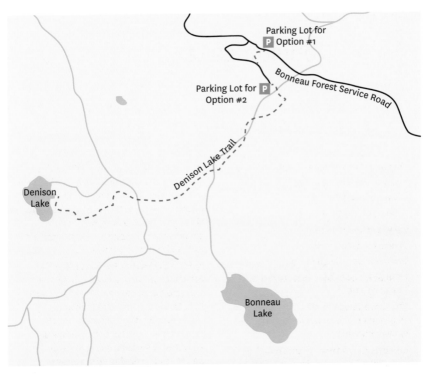

Creighton Creek on the hike in to Denison Lake.

the aforementioned boulder field, take the right fork.

6. For the most part, the remaining 2 km from the fork is level and is only interrupted by two noteworthy landmarks. At 3 km a bridge crosses Creighton Creek, and about 10 minutes before you reach the lake there is a boggy area that must be navigated by balancing on logs, poles and rocks carefully placed in the bog over many years by many travellers.

7. The shoreline of the gorgeous Denison Lake is attained in 4 km, or just over an hour from the cattle guard.

TOP: *The tranquil stillness of Denison Lake is worthy of a 2–3 hour round-trip hike.*

BOTTOM: *A small bridge crossing Bonneau Creek on the hike to Denison Lake.*

18 Adams River Trail to Adams River Gorge

This is an easy riverside walk with the reward of a spectacular view of the Adams River Gorge. The view is even more spectacular during spring runoff.

CATEGORY: Return

DISTANCE: 4 km round trip

HEIGHT GAIN: Nominal

HIGH POINT: 425 m

TIME: 1–2 hrs. round trip

DIFFICULTY: Moderate

SEASONS: Spring, summer, late fall

TRAILHEAD COORDINATES: N50 54 09.9 W119 35 18.2

DIRECTIONS TO TRAILHEAD: From the village of Chase, travel east on the Trans-Canada Highway for 10 km until you reach the turnoff to the North Shuswap region. This right-hand turn takes you onto the Squilax–Anglemont road. Drive this road for 4 km to reach a frontage road called Raft Pullout Rd. Park in the lot at the end of this short frontage road.

1. Walk around the yellow steel gate that spans a gravel road; this is the trailhead.

2. There is a very short climb right away, but this is the only climb on the trail.

3. The trail plateaus briefly before dropping back down to river level.

4. At the bottom of the hill, the trail splits. Go left, obeying the sign directing you to RIVER TRAIL.

5. Shortly after you've taken this left fork, the path opens into a large clearing, and within a few minutes it heads back into the cover of the forest.

6. The trail is wide and well travelled, an enjoyable stroll along the north bank of the Adams River.

7. At roughly 1 km into the hike, the first of two prominent lookouts veers slightly away from the trail, providing a spectacular view up the river. The second vantage point is another five minutes up the trail.

8. The path then leaves the riverside for a while, wandering into a forest of pine and spruce until it arrives at a fork approximately 2 km from the trailhead. Take the left fork, marked RIVER TRAIL AND CANYON.

9. The accessibility of the bluffs overlooking the gorge depends on water level and time of year. Your proximity to the rushing water as it funnels through the canyon is breathtaking, especially during high-water months. You are close enough to feel the spray, the pounding of the water and the slightest sensation of danger.

10. The River Trail that continues beyond the gorge is a 4 km walk, but the canyon is definitely the highlight. Regardless, this is not a loop trail, and you must return the same way you came.

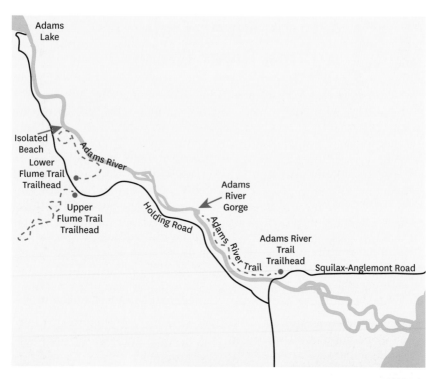

Adams Lake

Isolated Beach
Lower Flume Trail Trailhead
Adams River
Upper Flume Trail Trailhead
Holding Road
Adams River Gorge
Adams River Trail
Adams River Trail Trailhead
Squilax-Anglemont Road

TOP: *The spectacular Adams River from a lovely vantage point.*

BOTTOM: *The Adams River Gorge. A rich scenic reward for a moderate walk.*

OPPOSITE: *One of several viewpoints along the Adams River Trail.*

19 Lower Flume Trail

The Adams River was the landing point for massive logs that roared down a colossal 11-mile flume constructed nearly a century ago. These logs would reach speeds of 50 miles per hour down this V-shaped sluiceway. Although this is considered to be part of the historic Flume Trail, there doesn't appear to be any evidence of the flumes themselves. What it does provide is an incredible walk through an immense forest of huge trees unlike any in the British Columbia Interior, a wonderful walk along the fast-moving waters of the Adams River and a beautifully secluded beach created by the river's back eddy currents.

CATEGORY: Return with small loop

DISTANCE: 4 km round trip

HEIGHT GAIN: Nominal

HIGH POINT: 426 m

TIME: 1.5–2 hrs. round trip

DIFFICULTY: Moderate

SEASONS: Late spring, summer, late fall

TRAILHEAD COORDINATES: N50 55 14.4 W119 38 34.8

DIRECTIONS TO TRAILHEAD: From the village of Chase, travel east on the Trans-Canada Highway for 10 km until you reach the turnoff to the North Shuswap region. This right turnoff from the highway takes you onto the Squilax–Anglemont road. From the Squilax bridge, across the Little River, drive the Squilax–Anglemont road for 3 km and turn left on Holding Rd. Carry on along Holding Rd. for 5 km and pull into the parking area on the right side of the road. The trailhead is obvious, as signage for Lower Flume Trail directs you into a forest.

1. Most of this hike is a walk among giants. Monster cedar and hemlock trees throughout this journey are astounding, and the timespan of this trek depends on how enchanted you are by these magnificent Goliaths. Stop and look up as often as your neck muscles will allow.

2. About 10 minutes into the hike, you confront the first minor fork in the trail. While it may be tempting to continue straight down a well-trodden path, turn left onto the bridge instead. The fork that carries on straight quickly comes to an end as it meets water.

3. After crossing the bridge, the path comes head-on to a small offshoot of the Adams River a few short minutes later. Here, the trail T-splits. Take the left fork and parallel the west shoreline of the Adams River.

4. At the 2 km (30-minute) mark of the journey a trail branches to the left at a 90° angle. Continue straight along the riverside, and five minutes later you will pop out of the forest into a solid rock clearing. Below you is a torrential back eddy caused by the very rock outcropping you are standing on. This swirling action has fashioned a fabulous beach about 15 to 20 metres wide, with a depth that varies with the water level.

5. You can return the same way or complete a small loop that reconnects with the trail at a point you passed five minutes before you arrived at the beach. The trail is marked

TOP: *The single-track Lower Flume Trail wanders through a beautiful green forest.*

BOTTOM: *A small tributary makes its way to the Adams River.*

with cairns where it leaves the beach to enter the forest, and it climbs slightly uphill for a couple of minutes. Turn left when you approach a grass-covered road, and a minute of walking down this road will bring you to a left turn down a trail that puts you back on the main riverside trail. Turn right and head back to the trailhead.

See map on page 70.

TOP: *The payoff for hiking the Lower Flume Trail is this secluded beach and calm back eddy.*

BOTTOM: *The Lower Flume Trail sporadically parallels the rumbling Adams River.*

20 Upper Flume Trail

Although this is called an historic trail, actual artifacts are sparse. Some old moss-covered beams and a box of tin relics are found at the side of the trail at the far end of the upper loop at the END OF TRAIL sign. The interpretive sign at the trailhead describes the immensity of the undertaking of building an 11-mile-long, 5-foot-wide log flume. As the demand for more giant trees grew, logging companies ventured deeper into the forest, as the easy-picking riverside trees had all been plucked.

CATEGORY: Return, with small loops

DISTANCE: 4–6 km round trip

HEIGHT GAIN: Nominal, with one set of switchbacks

HIGH POINT: 534 m

TIME: 1.5–2 hrs. round trip

DIFFICULTY: Moderate

SEASONS: Late spring, summer, late fall

TRAILHEAD COORDINATES: N50 55 15.3 W119 38 38.1

DIRECTIONS TO TRAILHEAD: From Chase, travel east on the Trans-Canada Highway for 10 km until you reach the turnoff to the North Shuswap region. This right-hand turnoff takes you onto the Squilax–Anglemont road. From the Squilax bridge crossing the Little River, drive the Squilax–Anglemont road for 3 km to Holding Rd. and turn left. Carry on along Holding Rd. for 5 km and again turn left into the Upper Flume Trail parking lot on the left side of the road.

1. There are two trails entering the park, both beginning at this same parking lot. One heads to the right (west), while the other goes straight ahead through a gate of horizontal wood beams. When we last completed this hike, however, the west entrance to the trail system was closed and the trail to the right was suitably marked with a big yellow sign informing you of this. The reason for the closure was that the bridge marking the beginning of the trek is dilapidated and consequently unsafe. In fact, every bridge you cross on this journey is dilapidated, though the rest are still safe. The trail network consists of loops and criss-crossing trails that are well marked. The route described in this guide will deliver you to the end of the trail (actually the far reach of a loop) and will cross itself a couple of times. This particular course was chosen to provide maximum distance and hiking experience without the necessity of backtracking at the closed bridge at the trailhead.

2. So, pass through the wood-beam gate and parallel the peaceful waters of a creek that has two concurrent names: Hiuihill and Bear. The official toponym is Hiuihill Creek, but I think the Bear name likely got adopted because it's easier to pronounce, or maybe someone saw a bear in the creek at some point.

3. Seven to eight minutes into the hike, the path crosses the creek on an unstable bridge, the only significantly difficult part of the trek. The route begins to climb out of the narrow valley at the other side of the bridge. Switchbacks are the most dominant and conspicuous characteristic for the next

10 to 15 minutes. During this ascent, keep an eye out for Bear Creek Falls on the left side of the trail.

4. The switchbacks finally peak just over 1 km, or 15–20 minutes, into the hike. A sign reading UPPER TRAIL greets you at the summit of the climb. The sign has a single arrow pointing between the left and right forks – take the left fork. Look behind you to see a panorama of Tsalkom Mountain. Because the creek has a sudden drop in elevation at the falls, you are once again strolling alongside the creek. The creek is crossed a couple more times shortly after leaving the summit.

5. Roughly 2 km (30 minutes) from the trailhead, you encounter an intersection with two signs. Both have directional arrows pointing both left and right. One sign says TRAILHEAD, the other, LOOP TRAIL. Choose the right-hand, LOOP TRAIL path.

6. Five minutes later another junction presents another two signs, each with two bidirectional arrows: LOOP BACK TO TRAILHEAD and LOOP TO TOP OF TRAIL. Follow the latter sign, which is the right-hand fork.

7. In another five minutes you will arrive at a sign reading END OF TRAIL. This is actually not the end of the trail, but the far end of the upper loop. Here is where a few relics of the flumes remain. Moss-covered beams litter the forest here, and looking down the forest of scattered timbers you can see a clear path that appears to travel for several hundred metres.

8. The trail continues to loop, and five minutes from END OF TRAIL it meets another junction, this one with a sign saying LOOP BACK TO TRAILHEAD. Take the right-hand path. You have now hiked approximately 3 km. If you choose the left fork, it will take you to a maintained display consisting of a shortened replica of flume near a section of the original structure. As mentioned, the bridge is closed, so you will be required to backtrack, adding approximately 2 km to your day.

9. The remainder of the journey is obvious. Follow the signs to the trailhead, returning by the same way you came, and you will find your way back to the parking lot in another half-hour, for a total of 5 km.

See map on page 70.

TOP: *This area (Lower and Upper Flume Trails) is privileged to have such an abundance of these coniferous giants.*

BOTTOM: *Moss-covered beams from the 100-year-old log flume litter the forest floor.*

OPPOSITE: *The Upper Flume Trail.*

TOP: *Hiuihill Creek, also known as Bear Creek, is a prominent feature of this wondrous day hike.*

BOTTOM: *Beautiful Hiuihill Creek passes over many obstacles as it slowly makes its way to the Adams River.*

21 Tsútswecw Provincial Park

Tsútswecw Provincial Park is world-renowned for its spectacular sockeye salmon spawning grounds. Every four years, when the spawn reaches its zenith, the river banks are alive with spectators. And bears. The next dominant run in the Adams River is expected to occur in 2022. The salmon run usually happens during the first three weeks in October. Although this network of trails and bridges was designed and built to accommodate the throng of salmon-run visitors, it is a pleasant 6.7 km stroll at any time of year. The entire network is well marked and easily navigated.

CATEGORY: Return, with some small loops

DISTANCE: 6.7 km as single loop
Island Loop adds 750 m
Groundwater Spawning Channel diversion adds 800 m

TOTAL DISTANCE: 8.25–9 km, depending on side trails and loops

HEIGHT GAIN: None

HIGH POINT: 362 m

TIME: 1.5–2.5 hrs., depending on side trails and loops

DIFFICULTY: Moderate

SEASONS: Early spring, summer, late fall

TRAILHEAD COORDINATES: N50 54 09.9 W119 35 18.2

DIRECTIONS TO TRAILHEAD: From the village of Chase, travel east on the Trans-Canada Highway for 10 km to the turnoff for the North Shuswap region. This right-hand exit cloverleafs you onto the Squilax–Anglemont road northbound. Drive this road for 4 km to reach a frontage road call Raft Pullout Rd. Park in the lot at the end of this short service road (one of several parking lots along the length of this riverside provincial park). The trailhead is toward the river, under the bridge.

1. The path begins as a quiet, flat, single-track trail that meanders along the north side of the Adams River amongst large western red cedar and hemlock as well as lodgepole pine. This terrain will remain consistent for the next 1.6 km to the park's main parking lot. Prior to reaching the main lot, you will come across a plaque dedicated to Roderick Haig-Brown, and just beyond the plaque is a bridge-crossing for an island loop trail. The island loop is an enjoyable 10-minute diversion from the main trail if you feel up for a side-jaunt.

2. The park's main parking lot is a few minutes past the island loop bridge.

3. Out in the parking lot, look for the signs labelled LOWER TRAILS, which will take you across to the east side of the lot to Phil Rexin Memorial Trail. This path will regain the forest stroll through cedar, pine and hemlock. This is a walk in a magnificent forest with no sign of a river for 1.5 km until you reach a small bridge that crosses a minor stream.

4. A few minutes past the bridge, the trail meets a junction. The main loop continues on the left fork, while the right branch will take you to a closer look at the groundwater spawning channel. Another 500 m farther

TOP: *Regardless of the absence of spawning salmon during the summer months, Tsútswecw Provincial Park is a beautiful summertime stroll.*

BOTTOM: *The main parking lot for Tsútswecw Provincial Park was empty on this particular day.*

OPPOSITE: *The forest of western hemlock and cedar thins out as you approach a spawning channel on the left side of the trail.*

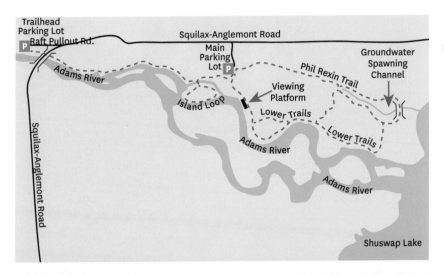

along, the trail encounters another fork; stay left again. Going right will return you to the groundwater spawning channel trail. Staying left at both intersections brings you back to the river and viewing platforms, and eventually back to the main parking lot, completing a 2 km walk from the bridge.

5. There is a variety of minor side trails, loops and bridges used for watching the spawning salmon in the river, its back eddies and resting pools, but the way is always conspicuous and specified with signage, always directing you back to the main parking lot.

6. At the main parking lot, find your way back from where you came on the trail to the Adams River bridge.

TOP: *The Adams River flows slowly through Tsútswecw Provincial Park.*

BOTTOM: *One of the many spawning grounds in the park.*

22 Fly Hills Recreation Area Lookout

This easy hike presents remarkable vistas of Salmon Arm, Shuswap Lake, Mount Ida and the Salmon River Valley. There is an optional, nearly vertical climb which can transform this route into a moderately strenuous one.

CATEGORY: Return or Loop

DISTANCE: 3–4.5 km round trip, depending on route chosen

HEIGHT GAIN: 66–161 m, depending on route chosen

HIGH POINT: 826 m

TIME: 1–2 hrs., depending on route chosen

DIFFICULTY: Moderate or Moderately strenuous, depending on route chosen

SEASONS: Late spring, summer, fall

TRAILHEAD COORDINATES: N50 40 41.8 W119 22 36.0

DIRECTIONS TO TRAILHEAD: Getting to the trailhead is more difficult than the trek itself in this instance, so here are step-by-step directions.

Travelling west on the Trans-Canada Highway from Salmon Arm, turn left on Salmon River Rd. about 3–4 km from downtown. Salmon River Rd. quickly becomes 10th Ave. SW. As it makes a sharp left turn the road becomes 50th St. SW. Very shortly after driving down 50th St. SW, turn right onto 13th Ave. SW (also known as Christison Rd.). Continue on this road for 1.3 km and turn left onto 5th Ave. After a brief 300 m on 5th Ave., turn left onto 60th St. In 700 m 60th St. will become 15th Ave. SW as it takes a 90° right turn. A little more than a kilometre later the road becomes Fly Hills FSR 170. Pavement soon gives way to gravel and 1 km later you'll see the parking lot on the left.

Now, the last time I drove this route (autumn of 2012), there were nice big, brand-new blue signs, with images of snowmobiles, directing traffic to the Fly Hills Recreation Area. This approach route would be much easier if those signs were permanent, but they weren't there in the spring of 2012 or 2011, so they may be only temporary in preparation for snowmobile season.

1. The way is not hard to find. The trail is a continuation of the forest service road, but it has been closed to motorized traffic (other than snowmobiles). Immediately into the hike the scenery will captivate you. You have already driven a substantial ascent, so seeing views that would normally require countless switchbacks becomes effortless.

2. Within 10 minutes you cross a small stream, and shortly after that there is an intersection where one road departs downhill to the left. You want to stay up high, so continue on the right fork.

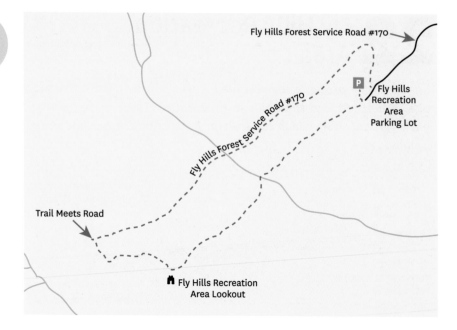

3. After another 10 to 15 minutes of mild elevation gain the trail comes to a large clearing that generally acts as the vantage point for most sightseers. This green clearing is 1.5 km from the parking lot.

4. There are now a few options:

a. You can take some amazing pictures and then turn around and head back to your vehicle.

b. For better viewing and to get some exercise, you can find the narrow, very steep trail on the back side of the clearing and climb for 5–10 minutes to reach a level stretch on the path.

c. Beyond the level section you can climb an awfully vertical section that lasts for another 5–10 minutes before popping out onto the forest service road. You can turn right to complete a loop trip, ambling downhill for 2.2 km to the parking lot.

5. The distance from the viewpoint below up to the forest service road is just over 500 m. The elevation gained is 95 m. Elevation gained from the parking lot to the main lookout is 66 m over a 1.5 km distance.

TOP: *A small stream crosses the road as it makes its way to the Salmon River Valley.*

BOTTOM: *Mount Ida seen from the Fly Hills Recreation Area Lookout.*

TOP: *The Fly Hills trail is mostly devoid of large trees, enabling great views of the region's mountains and valleys.*

BOTTOM: *A glimpse of Shuswap Lake and the town of Salmon Arm from the Fly Hills Recreation Area Lookout.*

23 Hyde Mountain Lookout

This hike takes you through a combination of thick forest and open meadows, with rewards of tremendous views.

CATEGORY: Return

DISTANCE: 15 km round trip

HEIGHT GAIN: 435 m

HIGH POINT: 917 m

TIME: 4–5 hrs. round trip

DIFFICULTY: Moderately strenuous

SEASONS: Late spring, summer, early fall

TRAILHEAD COORDINATES: N50 49 53.5 W119 00 07.3

DIRECTIONS TO TRAILHEAD: Drive west on the Trans-Canada Highway from the town of Sicamous and cross the Sicamous Narrows bridge (also known as the R.W. Bruhn bridge). There is an unnamed gravel road on the south (left) of the highway, 1 km beyond the west side of the bridge, just where the WELCOME TO SICAMOUS sign is. If traffic is heavy, continue a few kilometres up the highway, to where there are a few pullouts. Pull over on the right and return toward Sicamous when safe to do so. Coming from Salmon Arm, the unnamed gravel road is 6.5 km past 112 FSR.

Turn onto this road and immediately you will be greeted with a sign that reads PRIVATE DRIVE EXCEPT FOR TRAIL USERS. The local residents have graciously permitted us to enjoy the use of their driveway to satisfy our habit. The road splits 200 m later, and the right branch is the obvious way to go. Another 200 m later, the road finds its way to the parking lot. Please obey the signs and park without blocking driveways.

1. Signage at the trailhead sends you upward to the Larch Hills Traverse. Although directional signs to Hyde Mountain Lookout are not evident until much later in the trip, this is definitely the correct trail. It originates as a continuous climb among a forest of western red cedar and western hemlock. The forest floor changes from deadfall to rich green mosses and lichens as the trail progresses upward.

2. For the first 4 km of this trek, the trail ascends steadily, gaining 361 m, but this is not an ordinary series of switchbacks. These are perhaps the best-engineered switchbacks I have ever climbed. The distances between them are long and you barely notice the gradient, allowing you to catch your breath before you lose it. I was able to complete this 4 km with 361 m of elevation gain in just over an hour.

3. There is only one marker during this climb, at 3.5 km, indicating a viewpoint off the left side of the trail.

4. Just before completing the fourth kilometre you will approach a small clearing. The trail pops up out of the clearing to an old forest service road. A marker on a carefully planted post tells you to go left along the Larch Hills Traverse. This section of the traverse is a 40 km trail linking Salmon Arm with Sicamous, and is used by both hikers and cyclists.

5. A kilometre of wandering on a level, decommissioned forest service road brings you to the next post with markers. This is at a junction where another road merges from the right. Continue going straight as the marker suggests, following the GAME TRAIL SECTION.

6. The path continues as a pleasant, grassy

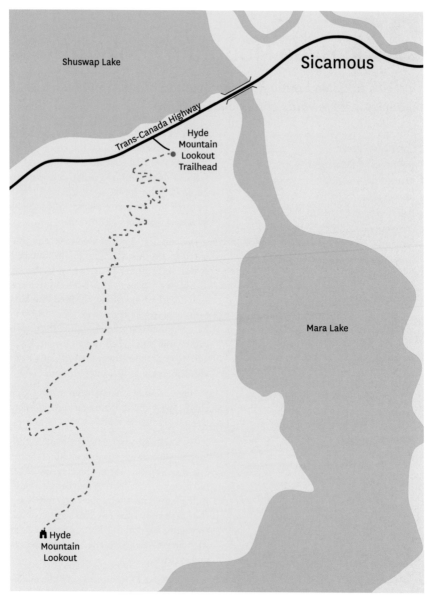

road, climbing steadily around an old cut-block. As the road flattens, it grazes a small clearing on its right side, with a secondary road veering off to the left. Another post, this one with a marker directing you up this secondary road to Hyde Mountain Lookout, is planted in plain sight.

7. Ten minutes on this road delivers you to a large clearing, maintaining its course on the right side of the clearing. As the road exits the clearing it narrows, and the vegetation closes in, becoming almost claustrophobic.

8. There is still almost another kilometre

TOP: *Many trails in this guidebook make use of old, deactivated logging roads.*

BOTTOM: *Does moss really grow only on the north side of trees? In this case, it was found on the north, east, west and south sides.*

TOP: *A delightful meadow on the Hyde Mountain Lookout trail allows sights of far-off mountains.*

BOTTOM: *Worth the journey. A spectacular view of Mara Lake seen from the Hyde Mountain Lookout.*

of hiking, and it's not a simple stroll in the woods, as the trail presents moments of upward labour.

9. The trail progressively narrows until it finally comes to an unexpectedly abrupt end. A faint single-track path continues beyond the road's end, immediately taking you to a fabulous viewpoint. Mara Lake is the unmistakable star featured from this vantage spot, with Black Point jutting out into the middle of the lake.

24 Larch Hills Nordic Trail Centre

Although scenery is limited, this is a wonderful spot for a long, easy, uninterrupted walk in the woods. Trail routes are numerous, it is far from the madding crowd and there is negligible elevation gain. This trail is probably one of the widest I have ever hiked.

CATEGORY: Loop

DISTANCE: 4.7 km on a loop trail

HEIGHT GAIN: Nominal

HIGH POINT: 1096 m

TIME: 2.5 hrs. including a few stops

DIFFICULTY: Moderate

SEASONS: Late spring, summer, fall

TRAILHEAD COORDINATES: N50 42 31.4 W119 08 08.3

DIRECTIONS TO TRAILHEAD: From downtown Salmon Arm, travel east on the Trans-Canada Highway, up a hill, to Highway 97B. Turn right onto 97B and drive south for 8.5 km to Grandview Bench Rd. Turn left onto Grandview Bench Rd. and after 5.5 km turn left again, onto Edgar Rd. Follow the signs to Larch Hills Nordic Centre for 6 km, arriving at a large parking lot.

1. It is evident that you could spend several days exploring this 125 km network of trails. The route I have chosen, comprising many equally relaxing trails, is almost a two-hour loop that skirts the lower western boundary of the system and comes home down the middle of it.

2. Heading north out of the parking lot, with the lodge on your right, you will immediately come to a fork in the road. Take the left split, called Metford Rd. (the right-hand fork is Larch Hills Rd.).

3. In the first 10 minutes, a couple of roads join Metford Rd., but the way is obvious.

At the 10-minute mark you will pass a yellow steel gate on the left directing you in to Bilbo's Bog. Stay on Metford Rd.

4. From the gate, over the next 10 minutes, Skyview and Raven's Ridge trails approach from the left. Once again, stay on the main road.

5. Look closely for Mushroom Fantasy Trail as it departs Metford Rd. to the right, 2 km, or 30 minutes, from the trailhead. Follow Mushroom Fantasy for about 1 km until it meets Ermine Frolic Loop about 15 minutes later. Take the left option to travel along Ermine Frolic Loop. From here on, the trail widens substantially.

6. Continue along the main road – it's unmistakable. This very wide, grassed-over road is a welcome respite from the many narrow, single-track trails in the Salmon Arm area. This is a fantastic way to walk through the woods; all this openness is rare in a forest stroll.

7. The Jay Walk path departs from Ermine Frolic Loop on its right side and will cut about 10 minutes off the trek. It is a lesser trail that cuts through the forest and reconnects with Ermine Frolic Loop about five minutes later. Alternatively, stick to Ermine Frolic Loop and make the full round of about 1 km.

8. Five minutes beyond the Jay Walk link with Ermine Frolic Loop, the trail travels through a rather large field. In the midst of this field, Ermine Frolic Loop goes both left and right; take the left option.

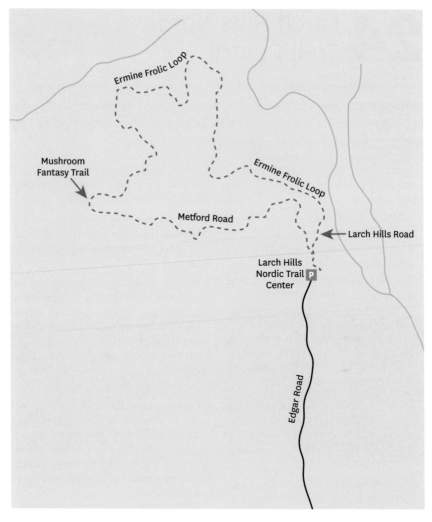

9. A few more trails continue to attach themselves to the main road for another 10 minutes until you reach the top of a steep downward hill. Don't worry, you're not going the wrong way on a one-way route, nor is it necessary for you to stay to the right side of the road. Those instruction signs are for the benefit of cross-country skiers.

10. Just beyond the bottom of the hill is Larch Hills Rd. Take the right fork to find yourself back at the parking lot within 5 to 10 minutes.

TOP: *The Larch Hills Nordic Trail Centre provides a network of forested trails. Many of them are quite wide, allowing for hiking with large groups of friends or family.*

OPPOSITE: *Large fungi growing on the forest floor.*

25 South Canoe Trail System

This trail system is the foremost mountain bike network at Salmon Arm, and although hiking is permitted on some of the routes, the wooded terrain requires you to be alert and prepared for bikers. There is an abundance of trails here and it would require an extensive amount of time to explore all of them, but the chief one used by hikers is the gravel service road (there's a radio tower 3 km up the road). This road is part of the extensive Larch Hills Traverse. The summit of this day hike is at about the 4 km mark.

CATEGORY: Return

DISTANCE: 10.6 km round trip

HEIGHT GAIN: 339 m

HIGH POINT: 937 m

TIME: 3–4 hrs. round trip

DIFFICULTY: Moderately strenuous

SEASONS: Late spring, summer, fall

TRAILHEAD COORDINATES: N50 41 33.9 W119 12 13.3

DIRECTIONS TO TRAILHEAD: Driving eastward on the Trans-Canada Highway through Salmon Arm, turn right (south) on Highway 97B. Travel 1.9 km on 97B and turn right onto 10th Ave. SE. Carry on for 1.5 km to the end of the road and a gravel parking lot.

1. The road continues through the parking lot, heading upward. It flattens periodically and the gradient varies for the first kilometre, but after that it is a moderate but persistent uphill incline. The trees open up from time to time, revealing spectacular sights of Shuswap Lake and surrounding hilltops.

2. Just past the 3 km mark, the road takes a sharp left turn. A secondary road exits to the right, but maintain your course on the main road going left. A radio tower stands on the left side, slightly past the apex of this turn.

3. Carrying on upward, the road enters a huge cutblock a few minutes later and begins to wind its way along the cutblock's far left (north) edge. After you've trudged 10–15 minutes along this boundary, the road plateaus as it reaches the summit of the cutblock.

4. Look for a bike trail sign reading SCHIZO on the right side of the road tacked high up on a topped tree. Although you have already been enjoying the wondrous views, they become richer as you move closer to the edge of the cutblock on the Schizo trail. You are at about the 4 km mark of the hike.

5. Farther down the trail, the view changes as the exposure to the south opens up more, although it is still somewhat obstructed. To better see the sights to the south, return to the main road and continue to a yellow 4.3 km marker. Take the right-hand fork here. Soon you will see the 5 km marker; continue for another 300 m or so until the forest on the right opens, exposing the valley below toward the south.

6. Return the same way.

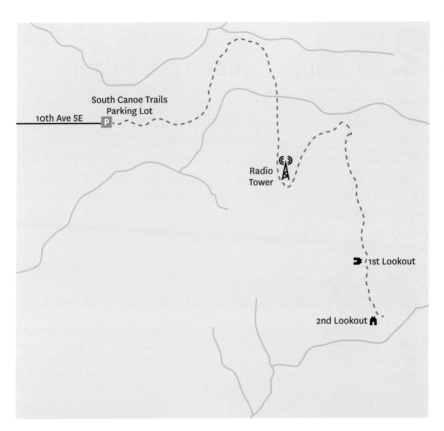

Many old forestry roads make fantastic hiking trails. This one takes you all the way to the best sights of the South Canoe Trail System.

TOP: *Trails criss-cross on the upper sections of the South Canoe Trail System. Pay attention to directional signs.*

BOTTOM: *Looking northwest from the main route of the South Canoe Trail System.*

26 Park Hill Trail System Outer Loop

This hike is the outer loop of a network known as the Park Hill Trail System within the city limits of Salmon Arm. It provides a cool, diverse forest walk with scenery that includes Shuswap Lake, with Sunnybrae Point and Bastion Mountain across the lake.

CATEGORY: Loop

DISTANCE: 3.5–4 km loop; side trails and viewpoints add to overall distance

HEIGHT GAIN: Nominal

HIGH POINT: 465 m

TIME: 1.5–2 hrs. round trip

DIFFICULTY: Moderate

SEASONS: Early spring, summer, late fall

TRAILHEAD COORDINATES: N50 45 20.8 W119 14 21.4

DIRECTIONS TO TRAILHEAD: From downtown Salmon Arm, take the Trans-Canada east. Turn left onto 30th St. NE and drive 4 km to 60th Ave. Turn right onto 60th Ave., which soon becomes Park Hill Rd. Drive another 2 km to the overflow parking for Canoe Beach, on the left. Park in the gravel lot.

1. The trailhead is easily found on the east end of the parking lot. The network is populated with shortcuts and quick trips, but to thoroughly enjoy this forest walk, follow the posted signs to the Outer Loop. Elevation is gained and lost throughout this walk, but there are no excruciating climbs, as the path simply undulates through a forest of birch, cedar and hemlock.

2. The first directional sign sends you to the left to pick up the Outer Loop East trail. The next five minutes presents a succession of signs as tributary trails branch off to the Koski parking area and Lund Trail. Continue to follow Outer Loop East Trail.

3. About 1 km from the trailhead, Outer Loop East Trail becomes Outer Loop South Trail.

4. Wander through the thick forest for another kilometre, enjoying the coolness that its canopy furnishes, passing junctions to Park Hill Rd. via Vye Trail, Sanson Trail via Hanna Trail and Sanson Trail via Petersen Trail and Ruth Trail.

5. Around the 2 km mark, Outer Loop South Trail becomes Outer Loop North Trail.

6. There are a couple of unmarked trails departing Outer Loop South and North, heading to the west (left). These trails go through private property, so please acknowledge the owners' privacy by treading lightly if you choose to take this short loop.

7. About five minutes on Outer Loop North, look for a narrow footpath that climbs slightly uphill to the left just as the lake comes into view. Take this short 10- to 15-minute divergence to Bastion Viewpoint to gain enhanced panoramas of Shuswap Lake and of course Bastion Mountain. From this viewpoint junction there is approximately 1.5 km remaining to the parking lot.

8. Returning from the Bastion Viewpoint to complete the Outer Loop North, you will notice some of the same trail names you encountered along Outer Loop South, now joining Outer Loop North from the right.

9. One of these routes on the right, presumably Lund Trail, is unmarked at a notable fork. Take the left branch and you will reach the parking lot in about 10 minutes.

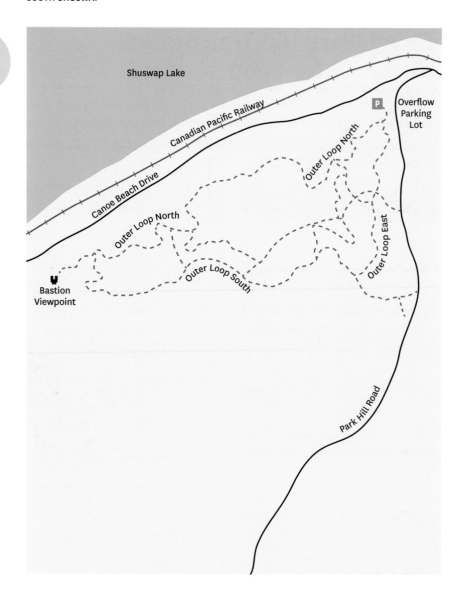

TOP: *A thick forest of western hemlock and cedar dominates the hike through the outer loop of the Park Hill Trail System.*

BOTTOM: *Glimpses of Shuswap Lake can be seen through the forest of the Park Hill system.*

TOP: *Bastion Mountain seen from the Bastion Viewpoint of the Park Hill Trail System.*

BOTTOM: *Shuswap Lake from the Bastion Viewpoint.*

27 Little Mountain Park

An abundance of criss-crossing trails characterizes the Little Mountain Park trail system. There are several different combinations of routes, but this one provides a lengthy outer excursion with an astonishing view of Shuswap Lake's Salmon Arm Bay, seen from the minor summit of Little Mountain.

CATEGORY: Loop

DISTANCE: 4 km loop around an 8 km trail system

HEIGHT GAIN: Nominal

HIGH POINT: 560 m

TIME: 1–1.5 hrs.

DIFFICULTY: Moderate

SEASONS: Spring, summer, fall

TRAILHEAD COORDINATES: N50 41 59.4 W119 14 41.4

DIRECTIONS TO TRAILHEAD: From downtown Salmon Arm, travel east on the Trans-Canada Highway, up the hill to 30th St. NE. Turn right and drive down 30th St. NE for 800 m and turn left on Okanagan Ave. The parking lot is at the end of the road, about 500 m away.

1. At the trailhead, take the right-hand branch of the first fork, and one minute later take the right-hand fork again.

2. Five minutes past this second junction, turn left to follow Larch Loop Trail for only a short distance before taking an immediate left onto Pine Trail. This short diversion takes you into a beautiful forest of larch and pine. These trails are marked with ample signage.

3. A short minute or so on Pine Trail leads you to Little Mountain Trail. A clearly displayed sign identifies the route, sending you to the right. The sign also confirms that you are heading toward the summit.

4. Five minutes of moderate climbing brings you to a minor, yet important, fork. Stay to the right, avoiding the SIDEHILL TRAIL TO 10TH AVE SE sign on the left. Sidehill Trail will deprive you of the spectacular views that are the main reason for this trek. Within a minute of walking up Little Mountain Trail, you reach the summit. A stunning panoramic view of Salmon Arm Bay is behind you as you reach the high point of this little mountain. A bench and picnic table accompany a communications tower at the top.

5. Continue past the tower to pick up the trail at the far end of the summit plateau, where it begins to descend.

6. In just a few minutes of walking downhill, you approach a couple of large water tanks on the opposite side of a wide gravel road. Turn right onto this road.

7. A gentle five-minute stroll down this road delivers you to the 10th Ave. parking lot.

8. Regain the trail as it leaves the parking lot and enters the forest, and follow the narrow path for about 4–5 minutes, obeying all signs that maintain your course on Outer Loop. Some of these signs are high up on trees, so when you're looking for them at intersections, look upward.

9. A fenced-in residence and a large field soon dominate the right side of the path for a hundred metres or so before you enter the forest again.

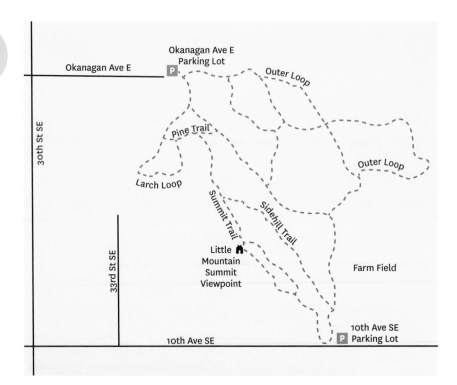

Okanagan Ave E
Okanagan Ave E Parking Lot
30th St SE
Outer Loop
Pine Trail
Larch Loop
Outer Loop
33rd St SE
Summit Trail
Sidehill Trail
Little Mountain Summit Viewpoint
Farm Field
10th Ave SE
10th Ave SE Parking Lot

ABOVE: *The aptly named Pine Trail of the Little Mountain Park system.*

OPPOSITE, TOP: *A large farmer's field in the midst of the Little Mountain Park trail network.*

OPPOSITE, BOTTOM: *Shuswap Lake seen from Little Mountain.*

10. Once you are back in the forest, the Outer Loop will keep you turning, because within the next 10 minutes you will meet approximately five forks in the trail. Monitor the signs on the trees and maintain your course on the Outer Loop Trail.

11. Enjoy these twists through the forest, as you will return to the starting point within 20 minutes from the farmer's field.

28 Salmon Arm Waterfront Trail
(including Salmon Arm Wharf Trail and Raven Trail)

Although this trek is situated in an urban area and parallels a railway track, it is truly an enlivening adventure, as it takes a trip through one of British Columbia's foremost migratory-bird estuaries. The combined Salmon Arm Wharf and Raven trails provide a gentle, level stroll that consists of elevated concrete walkways directly over the estuary along with viewing platforms, an elevated boardwalk and a loop around Christmas Island.

CATEGORY: Through

DISTANCE: 10.2 km round trip

HEIGHT GAIN: none

HIGH POINT: 359 m

TIME: 2.5–3 hrs. round trip

DIFFICULTY: Moderate

SEASONS: Early spring, summer, late fall, mild winters

TRAILHEAD COORDINATES FOR SALMON ARM WHARF TRAIL: N50 42 15.0 W119 17 04.2

TRAILHEAD COORDINATES FOR RAVEN TRAIL: N50 42 28.2 W119 16 21.1

DIRECTIONS TO TRAILHEAD: From the Trans-Canada Highway in downtown Salmon Arm, travel north on 4th St. NE for only a couple of blocks to where it intersects with Lakeshore Drive NE. Turn right on Lakeshore Drive NE and immediately get into the left-turn lane to cross the railway tracks onto Marine Park Drive NE. Turn left on Harbour Front Dr. NE and drive in front of the Prestige Harbourfront Resort & Convention Centre. Look for a parking spot on the road just past the resort. The unmistakable post and sign marking the beginning of Salmon Arm Wharf Trail stands on the right side of the road.

If you choose not to participate in the 1.2 km (one way) wharf walk and want to avoid the hotel and the marina park, turn right on Harbour Front Dr. and drive to its end to a gravel parking lot. This is the head of Raven Trail.

1. From the Salmon Arm Wharf trailhead, the path begins as a raised concrete walkway that makes its way behind the back of the Prestige Resort and its patio lounge and bar. The scene looking out onto the flat estuary is amazing and the wildlife immediately draws you in. Late in the season, when the lake is low, the estuary gives the appearance of a tidal flat that should soon be overcome with an incoming tide, but this lake "tide" will not return until the spring. And as you can imagine, spring and early summer are when this estuary is teeming with life.

2. This is the first of two raised concrete walkways, and it lasts only for about five minutes. Cross Marine Park Drive NE and

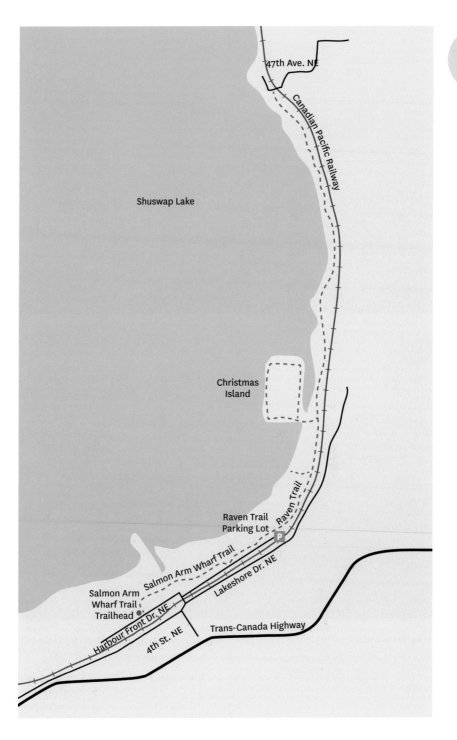

47th Ave. NE

Canadian Pacific Railway

Shuswap Lake

Christmas Island

Raven Trail

Raven Trail Parking Lot

Salmon Arm Wharf Trail

Lakeshore Dr. NE

Salmon Arm Wharf Trail Trailhead

Harbour Front Dr. NE

4th St. NE

Trans-Canada Highway

TOP: *This boardwalk exits the bush, taking you over marshy grasses and revealing fantastic scenery.*

BOTTOM: *These protected lands enable waterfowl to raise their young undisturbed.*

OPPOSITE: *A lengthy archway of birch and alder.*

pick up where the obvious sign stands on the other side of the road. Follow the concrete path as it winds its way around a parking lot to the next elevated concrete pathway. This second walkway is much longer and provides far superior viewing.

3. When this comes to an end, it takes a 90° right turn to Harbour Front Dr. NE. Turn left and hike the road a short distance to the Raven trailhead. Concrete now surrenders to dirt and gravel. This is a magnificent trail.

4. Within 5–7 minutes the first viewing platform is accessed on the left. This short jaunt projects you out of the forest, offering fantastic, unobstructed panoramas of this beautiful sanctuary.

5. One of the many amusing features of this easy, yet interesting trek is the overgrown birch and alder trees that have created lengthy archways, almost tunnel-like.

6. The trail to the Christmas Island loop is at about the 1 km mark from the Raven trailhead. This loop is 1.2 km long and is a worthy side trip, as it is the farthest extension out into the estuary.

7. Back on the main trail, continuing north, you come to the second viewing platform. This platform was closed in 2012, as the boardwalk out to it had severely deteriorated.

8. All along the way, the thin forest opens up, presenting spectacular sights, but some of the best views are seen from a sturdy boardwalk of about 100 to 150 m in length.

9. Beyond the boardwalk, the expedition lasts a further 15 minutes as it makes its way through high marsh growth.

10. The journey ends at 47th Ave. NE. Turn back and enjoy everything you missed the first time.

TOP: *At some points the Raven trail hugs the marshlands of Shuswap Lake.*

BOTTOM: *Christmas Island presents shoreline views of Shuswap Lake.*

29 Margaret Falls

This is by far the shortest hike in this guide, but it has some of the most interesting vegetation in the province. The falls are at the end of a closed canyon with high walls that allow only limited sunlight. The soil, the moisture from the falls and the canyon's ultraviolet shield are ripe growing conditions that have produced colossal trees, and the dominant variety here is cedar. Gigantic Douglas firs also inhabit the canyon. Both of these monsters are thick and tall. The moist canyon is a breeding ground for forest-floor species as well, including thimbleberry, mosses and foamflower.

CATEGORY: Return

DISTANCE: 1.5 km round trip

HEIGHT GAIN: Nominal

HIGH POINT: 380 m

TIME: 20–30 min. round trip; much longer if you absorb the experience

DIFFICULTY: Easy

SEASONS: Spring, summer, late fall

TRAILHEAD COORDINATES: N50 47 19.8 W119 12 22.5

DIRECTIONS TO TRAILHEAD: From downtown Salmon Arm, travel west on the Trans-Canada Highway for 15 km and turn right onto Sunnybrae Canoe Point Rd. Drive 11.2 km to arrive at the Margaret Falls parking lot, on the left side of the road. From the parking lot, follow the marked path to Margaret Falls, which initially heads downhill.

The interpretive trail is easy to follow, as it is railed with chain rope. The first sign you will read explains the purpose of the rails of chain: too many tourists have gone off-trail and trampled the delicate forest-floor ecosystem. Many have climbed the fragile trees that lean over the creek, wearing away the bark and leaving exposed, unprotected wood. Some visitors have even climbed the canyon walls, eradicating rare plants that cling there. In an effort to preserve this beautifully unique niche, it became essential to confine visitors to the trail.

The path shadows Reinecker Creek, crossing it about three times before reaching the falls. Of course, the water level varies significantly depending on the time of year, but the constant seems to be a slow, easy flow. Considering the noise and heartbeat pounding of the falls a short distance away, the leisurely passage of the stream fails to prepare you for what lies ahead.

As mentioned, the trees in this canyon are enormous. Several have fallen, yet even uprooted they insist on living; they lean on the canyon walls like huge ramps up to the rim. Most are broad, towering suppliers of abundant shade, rendering the stroll cool and dank, yet refreshing.

At the end of this short, fascinating journey the trail becomes a wooden platform, soaked from the constant spray of Margaret Falls. Be careful your camera doesn't get wet, and more importantly, watch your footing on the slippery planks.

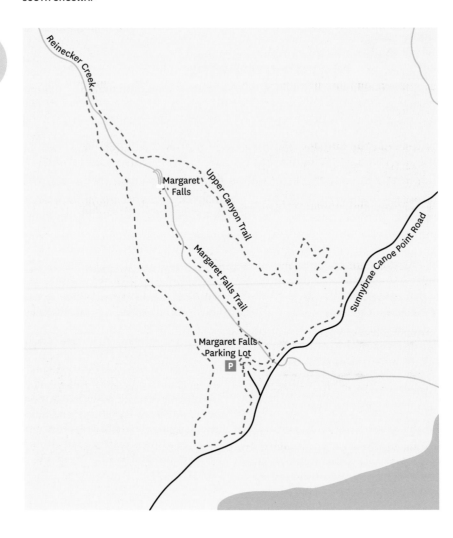

TOP: *The perpetually swift waters of Reinecker Creek eventually uproot many seemingly stable tall cedar trees.*

BOTTOM: *Gigantic cedars and Douglas firs stretch toward the upper rim of Reinecker Creek canyon (aka Margaret Falls canyon).*

TOP: *The spectacular Margaret Falls.*

BOTTOM: *Tyler Shea waits patiently on a bridge in the Margaret Falls canyon while his father takes pictures.*

30 Margaret Falls Upper Canyon Loop

This loop takes you up the east side of Reinecker Creek, crossing it on a narrow bridge far above the falls and finishing off with a stroll down the west side of the creek.

CATEGORY: Loop

DISTANCE: 2.5 km (does not include 650 m of paved road)

HEIGHT GAIN: 140 m

HIGH POINT: 522 m

TIME: 1–1.5 hrs. including 650 m of pavement

DIFFICULTY: Moderate

SEASONS: Spring, summer, fall

TRAILHEAD COORDINATES: N50 47 19.8 W119 12 22.5

DIRECTIONS TO TRAILHEAD: From downtown Salmon Arm, travel west on the Trans-Canada Highway for 15 km and turn right onto Sunnybrae Canoe Point Rd. Drive 11.2 km to arrive at Margaret Falls parking lot, on the left side of the road.

1. From the Margaret Falls parking lot, follow the path to Margaret Falls (this is the only trail leaving the parking lot). It makes its way downward and briefly parallels the paved road. Here you must leave the trail and jump up onto the road to continue approximately 400 m to a wooden staircase on the left side of the road. Make your way up this short set of steps to the trailhead of the Upper Canyon Loop.

2. The single-track trail begins to climb immediately and within 10 minutes produces a spectacular view of Shuswap Lake. Another five minutes later, there is a minor junction where a side trail diverts to a viewpoint. The main trail resumes to the right (straight).

3. Through a thick forest, the way takes you creekside among a forest of spruce and pine, with the rumble of Margaret Falls as a constant in the background. A half-hour into the hike the trail comes to its first key intersection. At this point, you have trekked 1.4 km from the wooden staircase off Sunnybrae Canoe Point Rd. The sign says that the west portion of the Upper Canyon Loop carries on straight and the Lower East Reinecker Creek Trail goes up a narrow trail to the right. Continue straight (left fork) and cross Reinecker Creek a couple of minutes later on a skilfully constructed wooden beam bridge.

4. Now on the west side of the creek, the path turns and makes its way back to the parking lot. It travels creekside as a wide, unobstructed trail, but within 10 minutes the trail is high above the creek as the creek makes its descent toward Margaret Falls.

5. For the next 15 minutes the route is a pleasant, flat stroll through a dense forest of western hemlock and western red cedar. The flat walk eventually drops down to the paved road, where you will turn left to make your way back to the parking lot, 250 m away.

See map on page 110.

TOP: *The Reinecker Creek bridge crossing at the zenith of Margaret Falls Upper Canyon Loop.*

BOTTOM: *The descent back to the Margaret Falls parking lot is mostly a pleasant, flat walk among gorgeous western red cedar and western hemlock.*

OPPOSITE, TOP: *The upward hike toward the Reinecker Creek bridge rises above Margaret Falls, heard below but not seen.*

OPPOSITE, BOTTOM: *This sensational vista of Shuswap Lake is seen within the first 15 minutes of the hike. This photo was taken at dawn.*

31 Reinecker Creek Lower Loop

CATEGORY: Loop

DISTANCE: 11.5 km (does not include 650 m of walking on paved road)

HEIGHT GAIN: 140 m

HIGH POINT: 764 m

TIME: 3–4 hrs. round trip, including 650 m of pavement

DIFFICULTY: Moderate

SEASONS: Spring, summer, fall

TRAILHEAD COORDINATES: N50 47 19.8 W119 12 22.5

DIRECTIONS TO TRAILHEAD: From downtown Salmon Arm, travel west on the Trans-Canada Highway for 15 km and turn right onto Sunnybrae Canoe Point Rd. Drive 11.2 km to arrive at the Margaret Falls parking lot, on the left side of the road.

1. From the parking lot, follow the path to Margaret Falls, which is the only trail leaving the parking lot. It makes its way downward and briefly parallels the paved road. Here you must leave the trail and jump up onto the road to continue for about 400 m to a wooden staircase on the left side of the road. Make your way up this short set of steps to the trailhead of the Upper Canyon Loop.

2. There needs to be some clarification at this point: these trails are under the care of two separate parties. The Upper Canyon Loop Trail is part of Herald Provincial Park and thus is maintained by BC Parks, while the Reinecker Creek system was built and is maintained by the Shuswap Trail Alliance. Thus the first 1.4 km of this route is in the provincial government's portion, and when you reach the 1.4 km mark the Reinecker Trail begins. So, although the sign at the trailhead says that LOWER EAST REINECKER CREEK TRAIL is 4.3 km in length, it is actually 5.7 km long if you count the additional 1.4 km.

3. The single-track trail begins to climb immediately and within 10 minutes produces a spectacular view of Shuswap Lake. Another five minutes later there is a minor junction where a side trail diverts to a viewpoint. The main trail resumes to the right (straight).

4. Through thick forest the way takes you creekside amid spruce and pine, with the rumble of Margaret Falls as a constant in the background. A half-hour into the hike the trail comes to its first key intersection. At this point you have trekked 1.4 km from the wooden staircase off Sunnybrae Canoe Point Rd. The sign says the west portion of Upper Canyon Loop carries on straight and the Lower East Reinecker Creek Trail goes up a narrow trail to the right. Although the sign back at the parking lot gave the distance to Lower East Reinecker Creek Trail as 4.3 km, the one at this junction claims it is 4 km. Regardless, clamber up the right fork of this junction.

5. For the next hour, the trail presents no obstacles; it does nothing other than ramble through an ever-changing forest of cedar, spruce, hemlock, alder and birch. But it's an enchanting forest and thus a totally enjoyable interval. The hour is interrupted by a minor bridge crossing over an insignificant stream after the trail descends briefly.

6. The path climbs just as briefly for about five minutes before passing through a wooden gate. Five minutes beyond the gate, the Upper East Reinecker Trail ends and you have the choice of taking South Crossing Trail to the left or Upper East Reinecker Trail to the right. Go left. As the

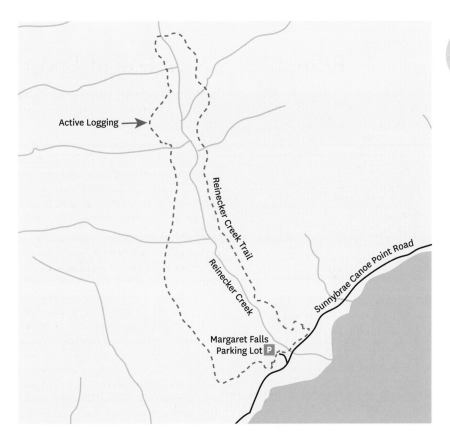

Active Logging →

Reinecker Creek Trail

Reinecker Creek

Sunnybrae Canoe Point Road

Margaret Falls
Parking Lot P

marker indicates, the South Crossing Trail is 1.2 km long. On this post, trail distances have been corrected with ink – more unnecessary confusion.

7. You will cross Reinecker Creek in another few minutes, putting you on the west side of the creek with almost a kilometre behind you from the previous bridge. The next 15 minutes (about 1 km) is a mixture of an undulating trail through forest, over boardwalks and alongside cutblocks.

8. Some 1.2 km from the last junction, the trail is split, with a marker directing you leftward down the Lower West Trail. You have now joined a multi-purpose decommissioned logging road that was in good use on my last trek along it. This trail ends, and so does your journey, in 4.5 km.

9. The next couple of kilometres are relatively uneventful until the forest opens up and you find yourself in the middle of an active logging zone. This is really quite fascinating, and as it is such a vital segment of the BC economy, there is a certain amount of awe when walking through one of hundreds of such zones throughout the province. So much machinery, labour and planning, and the impact on jobs is evident in cutblocks such as this. The Shuswap Trail Alliance has done a superb job of updating the posts with directional arrows in the midst of this dynamic, ever-changing logging landscape. In the spring of 2012 two such posts guided you safely within this area. This may change as the terrain is altered. At most, you should be through this landing within 10–15 minutes.

TOP: *You might think you would easily lose the trail in this mayhem of logging activity, but volunteers from the Shuswap Trail Alliance have done a magnificent job of marking the way through the confusion.*

BOTTOM: *Although the forest has been uprooted, it is humbling to see the grassroots activity of one of British Columbia's major economic powerhouses.*

10. Signage will drop you down to the left, back onto the main path, and once again your feet pound a trail of gentle, silent earth. After 10 minutes of strolling back through a forest, you find the first of five unmistakable signs placing you safely on Sunnybrae Canoe Point Rd.

11. Turn left on the pavement to regain the parking lot within a few short minutes.

32 Sunnybrae Bluffs

This area is a labyrinth of twisting trails, shortcuts and roads without a single directional sign. After a day of wandering, I have managed to make this easy for you. The elevation gain is minimal at 156 m and the distance is short, but the viewing at the summit is expansive.

CATEGORY: Return

DISTANCE: 4 km round trip

HEIGHT GAIN: 156 m

HIGH POINT: 520 m

TIME: 1 hr. round trip

DIFFICULTY: Moderately strenuous

SEASONS: Spring, summer, early fall

TRAILHEAD COORDINATES: N50 46 33.0 W119 18 00.7

DIRECTIONS TO TRAILHEAD: From downtown Salmon Arm, travel 15 km west on the Trans-Canada Highway and make a right turn onto Sunnybrae Canoe Point Rd. Drive 3.4 km and park in the Sunnybrae parking lot, on the right (lake) side of the road.

1. The trail starts across the road from the Sunnybrae parking lot. The trail is a single-width path that begins climbing immediately, but the climb only lasts for about five minutes. Shortly after the trail levels out, a narrower one approaches from the left. Both trails merge a short distance ahead.

2. The route soon enters a large clearing. The path is picked up at the far end of the clearing as an overgrown dusty road. Strolling along this road, enjoy the fantastic view of Shuswap Lake. You may also notice some residential housing below the embankment on your right.

3. A few short minutes later this overgrown road meets a gravel road coming up from the residential area. Turn left up this road, and within barely one minute take the first narrow path that leaves the gravel road on your left. This narrow shortcut starts to climb slightly.

4. Five to 10 minutes up this trail an additional trail approaches from the right – continue straight.

5. Another five to ten minutes later the trail connects with the original gravel road it departed from.

6. Soon after picking up the gravel road, the trail splits; make sure you take the left branch.

7. Within a few minutes you arrive at the summit of the bluffs and are presented with some of the most sensational scenery in this part of the planet. Be careful, though: the edge is steep and the drop is long.

8. If you feel like exploring a bit more, the trail continues as a wonderful ridge walk for 10 to 15 minutes, finally ending in a very large private farmer's field.

9. Return the same way.

TOP: *Shuswap Lake's Tappen Bay seen from Sunnybrae Cliffs looking north.*

BOTTOM: *Tappen Bay from Sunnybrae Cliffs looking south. Definitely a hike worthy of one hour out of your day.*

OPPOSITE: *This glorious field can be found 10 to 15 minutes beyond the Sunnybrae Cliffs viewpoint.*

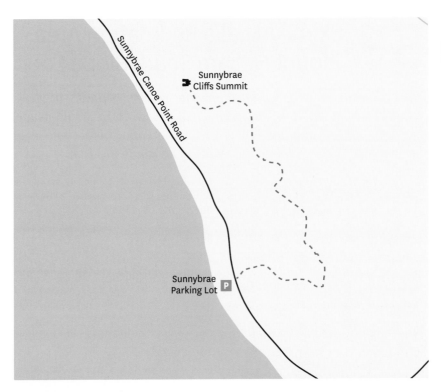

33 Skimikin Lake Recreation Area – Mount Hilliam South Slope Loop

This arduous and lengthy climb provides terrific bounties of views across the Skimikin Valley, Skimikin Lake, Shuswap Lake and neighbouring bluffs and peaks. It is noteworthy to mention before you begin this loop that there is a 4 km road walk to conclude this trek.

CATEGORY: Loop

DISTANCE: 16.2 km loop trip

HEIGHT GAIN: 527 m

HIGH POINT: 1090 m

TIME: 4.5–5.5 hrs. to complete the loop

DIFFICULTY: Strenuous

SEASONS: Late spring, summer, early fall

TRAILHEAD COORDINATES: N50 47 10.4 W119 26 18.7

DIRECTIONS TO TRAILHEAD: About 14 km west of Salmon Arm, on the Trans-Canada Highway, turn left (south) onto Tappen Valley Rd. Drive 4 km and turn left on Skimikin Rd. Travel 6 km along Skimikin Rd. to find the Skimikin Lake Recreation area off the left side of the road. The way from the highway is clearly marked with signage. Immediately upon arriving in the recreation area, you will find yourself in a large unpaved parking area. Park here.

1. Cross Skimikin Rd. and pick up the trail that parallels the paved road. Within five minutes the double-wide path veers upward to the right and becomes trail EQ 4.

2. Continue to follow the red EQ 4 markers, which are fastened to trees, as the path makes its way upward. The climbing has begun. A couple of minor trails intersect with EQ 4, but when these approach, don't deviate from the main path; the way is obvious.

3. About 2 km, or 30 minutes, into the hike, the forest opens, allowing the hills you are climbing to come into view. Around the same time, the path reaches a four-way intersection. Continue a straight course, ignoring the trails that approach from the left and the right.

4. EQ 4 now becomes EQ 16. A red marker attached to a tree on the right side of the path will confirm this for you. A few minutes on EQ 16 brings you to a young forest and a sign indicating that this youth was planted in 2000. The trail ascends steadily on a mild gradient.

5. Ten minutes of steady upward motion delivers you to a magnificent, wide-open, level clearing surrounded by mature birch trees.

6. Once the trail emerges from the birch-lined clearing it resumes its relentless upward journey to its high destination.

7. Slightly more than 15 minutes farther on, the path meets a key junction. Trail EQ 22 arrives from the left and cuts across the top of EQ 16, ending its journey. At this T intersection, large arrows guide you out of the trail system, giving you the choice of either right or left. Turn left onto EQ 22 and continue to climb this slow, steady slope. You have now hiked approximately 3.5–4 km. Just so you know what you're in for, the seemingly endless elevation gain continues for almost another hour, relieved by only a couple of brief plateaus.

8. Roughly 1 km after you join EQ 22, the tree line breaks and the panoramas up and down the Skimikin Valley are revealed. As you look to the far left (northeast),

Birch trees in the midst of a coniferous forest create a lovely mixture of foliage.

Shuswap Lake and Notch Hill dominate the view, but the most visible landmark is Skimikin Lake directly below.

9. You will still continue to climb for another half-hour or so, and just before the path finally flattens, a small sign reminds you that you are still on EQ 22. Where the trail levels, trail EQ 34 approaches from the right. EQ 22 comes to an end as it merges into EQ 34.

10. You have now clambered up 527 m of elevation gain. Congratulations! The trail flattens for a short distance before it begins its drop back down to Skimikin Rd.

11. Within 10 minutes of downhill hiking, you'll come to a significant gravel road. Turn left onto it. You are now about 7.5 km, or two hours, into the hike.

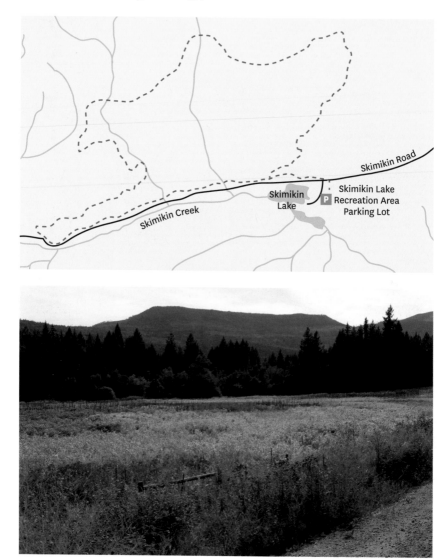

124

TOP: *The eastward view from the south slope of Mount Hilliam.*

BOTTOM: *Looking west from high up the south slope.*

OPPOSITE: *A 4 km return walk on a gravel road from exploring the south slopes of Mount Hilliam is enhanced by the sights, sounds and smells of a marshy swamp and a slow-moving stream.*

TOP: *Skimikin Lake viewed from the south slope of Mount Hilliam.*

BOTTOM: *Small lakes relinquish much of their water on hot summer days. Skimikin is no exception.*

OPPOSITE: *A roadside view of Skimikin Lake.*

12. Five to ten minutes down the gravel road, a PRIVATE PROPERTY sign is highly visible. It is okay to stay on the road, but do not wander onto the property. Viewing at this point is exceptional as you amble down a superb, vast, open slope.

13. Slightly more than a kilometre down the gravel road, a well-marked junction with trail EQ 30 sends you off the road and into the forest to the right, where you immediately cross a stream. This is an important crossroad, because the gravel road continues down to private property. This diversion around private property is the reason why there is a 4 km hike back to the parking lot on Skimikin Rd.

14. After eight to ten minutes on EQ 30 you'll come to a small clearing that has an unmarked trail on your left. Take this unmarked trail to where it joins with EQ 28 just a few minutes farther along. Turn left on EQ 28.

15. The next kilometre is a walk on an overgrown double-track road that weaves in and out of forest and meadow. The trail will eventually come to a locked fence, on the other side of which is the same stream you crossed 45 minutes ago.

16. From here the trail becomes EQ 24 and it will take you down to Skimikin Rd. in about 20 minutes.

17. Turn left on Skimikin Rd. and enjoy a 4 km hike back to the parking lot. The landscape on the right side of the road is fed with the slow, even stagnant waters of Skimikin Creek. Patches of marsh and wetland are prevalent where the running water has pooled.

34 Skimikin Lake Recreation Area – East View Loop

A forest walk with open vistas and a creekside stroll.

CATEGORY: Loop

DISTANCE: 5.7 km round trip

HEIGHT GAIN: Nominal

HIGH POINT: 666 m

TIME: 1.5–2 hrs. round trip

DIFFICULTY: Moderate

SEASONS: Spring, summer, late fall

TRAILHEAD COORDINATES: N50 47 10.4 W119 26 18.7

DIRECTIONS TO TRAILHEAD: About 14 km west of Salmon Arm, on the Trans-Canada Highway, turn left (south) onto Tappen Valley Rd. Drive 4 km and turn left on Skimikin Rd. Travel 6 km along Skimikin Rd. to find the Skimikin Lake Recreation area off the left side of the road. The way from the highway is clearly marked with signage.

1. Immediately upon arriving in the recreation area, you will find yourself in a large unpaved parking area. Continue through this lot and pick up the main road at the other end. Carry on for about 400 m to the day use area near the lake. Park anywhere near the picnic tables.

2. You are at the trailhead in the day use parking area, so your journey can begin as soon as you are ready. Facing the lake, walk along the main road to your left (east). A marker up on a tree in the day use area will indicate you are on trail #8. You want to get to the far southeast end of the lake and enter the surrounding forest. Depending on the water level, there are two roads you can take that wrap around the far end of the lake. It should only take five minutes to walk past the lakeside campsites and enter the forest.

3. Once in the forest, you'll encounter a network of roads almost immediately, so pay attention. First, the two roads that bypass the lake intersect. Momentarily you meet another road, with three stacked signs nailed to a tree. Fortunately they all exhibit the same singular instruction: OUT. Although #8 trail is marked on a tree looking down the left fork, follow the OUT, OUT, OUT trail to the right, as you eventually want to arrive on trail #10.

4. Immediately, you approach another junction – take the left fork.

5. Thirty seconds later, at the intersection with #10 trail, turn left, staying on #10. This is an old, overgrown road, which makes for easy walking. The next 20–25 minutes of the hike is easily navigable and enjoyable. With the exception of a brief incline, the road is flat, wide and open, offering panoramas of Mount Hilliam 4.3 km to the northwest (look left as you walk).

6. Approximately 2.5 km from the trailhead, the path arrives at a narrow, trickling, soothing creek and a primary gravel forestry road. The #10 trail diverts downhill to the left just before reaching the creek. Walk downward among a mixed forest of cedar, pine and birch, accompanied by the slow-moving creek. Of course, in the Okanagan the level of water in streams like this depends on the amount of runoff that year and how early in the season you are hiking.

7. Five to 10 minutes down this pleasant path the #8 trail appears to the left. Take the left turn and follow the #8 back to Skimikin Lake.

8. For the next kilometre, the trail dodges in and out of the forest as it parallels a tall wire fence on your right. Beyond the fence, large fields and tree islands make up the British Columbia Skimikin Seed Orchards.

9. Eventually the fence ends and the forest takes over. About five to ten minutes beyond the fenceline you will return to the three OUT signs. Turn right and make your way back to the Skimikin day use area.

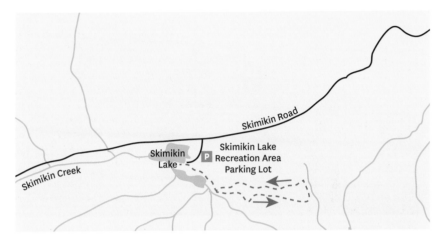

The trail breaks free of the forest to allow such scenery of the surrounding hillsides.

TOP: *The Skimikin Lake eastern trails open through the forest to many spectacular sights.*

BOTTOM: *An area previously logged of its riches allows young trees to prosper.*

35 Skimikin Lake to Granite Creek Estate Winery

A forest walk with open vistas and a rest stop at a winery.

CATEGORY: Loop and Return combined

DISTANCE: 12.4 km round trip

HEIGHT GAIN: Nominal

HIGH POINT: 666 m

TIME: 3–3.5 hrs. round trip

DIFFICULTY: Moderate

SEASONS: Spring, summer, late fall

TRAILHEAD COORDINATES: N50 47 10.4 W119 26 18.7

DIRECTIONS TO TRAILHEAD: About 14 km west of Salmon Arm, on the Trans-Canada Highway, turn left (south) onto Tappen Valley Rd. Drive 4 km and turn left on Skimikin Rd. Travel 6 km along Skimikin Rd. to find the Skimikin Lake Recreation area off the left side of the road. The way from the highway is clearly marked with signage. Immediately upon arriving in the recreation area, you will find yourself in a large unpaved parking area. Continue through this lot and pick up the main road at the other end. Carry on for about 400 m to the day use area near the lake. Park anywhere near the picnic tables.

1. You are at the trailhead in the day use parking area, so your journey can begin as soon as you are ready. Facing the lake, walk on the main road to your left (east). A marker up on a tree in the day use area will indicate you are on trail #8. You want to get to the far southeast end of the lake and enter the surrounding forest. Depending on the water level, there are two roads to take that wrap around the far end of the lake. It should only take five minutes to walk past lakeside campsites and enter the forest.

2. Once in the forest, you encounter a network of roads almost immediately, so pay attention. First, the two roads that bypass the lake intersect. Momentarily another road is met, with three stacked signs nailed to a tree. Fortunately they all exhibit the same singular instruction: OUT. Although the #8 trail is marked on a tree looking down the left branch, follow the OUT, OUT, OUT trail to the right, as you eventually want to arrive on trail #10.

3. Immediately, you approach another junction. Take the left fork.

4. Thirty seconds later, at the intersection with #10 trail, turn left, staying on #10. This is an old, overgrown road, which makes for easy walking. The next 20–25 minutes of the hike is easily navigable and enjoyable. With the exception of a brief incline, the road is flat, wide and open, giving panoramas of Mount Hilliam 4.3 km to the northwest (look left as you walk).

5. Approximately 2.5 km from the trailhead, the path arrives at a narrow, trickling, soothing creek and a primary gravel forestry road. The #10 trail diverts downhill to the left just before reaching the creek.

6. Cross the stream and turn left to descend down the road for about a kilometre to where the road levels off and takes a sharp left turn. This juncture is well marked with various signs. One is a yellow mileage indicator marked "0 160"; another tells us we are in the Fly Hills snowmobile area; the third warns us we are in a wilderness watch area.

7. At the apex of the curve in the road, a narrow trail darts off into the trees to the right. Once you're into the forested trail, a #10 marker is visible on a tree. Follow this trail through a dark forest for about 3 km to reach the winery.

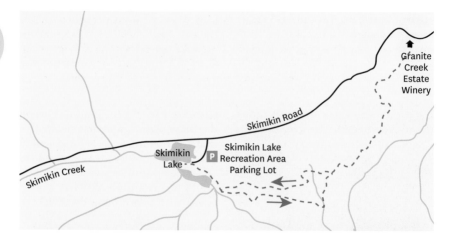

8. For the most part, the way is clear and marked with small #10 signs. Near the end, however, the trail hits an unmarked junction where one fork continues straight and has a significantly steep upward grade. Take the right fork and within five minutes the path emerges onto a gravel road.

9. Turn left onto the gravel road and within another five minutes you will arrive at the winery.

10. Return the same way, but when you reach the gravel road with the three signs, turn right instead of heading back up the road. Some 30 or 40 m along the road you will notice a path leading into the forest on the left (south) side. Once you are in the forest, markers on a tree make it evident that you are on the combined trails #10 and #8. Follow this path through the bush for about five minutes until #8 takes a right turn and #10 continues straight up to the creek crossing. Turn right onto trail #8 to return to Skimikin Lake.

11. For the next kilometre, the trail dodges in and out of the forest as it parallels a high wire fence on your right. Beyond the fence, large fields and tree islands make up the British Columbia Skimikin Seed Orchards.

12. Eventually the fence ends and the forest takes over. About five to ten minutes beyond the fenceline you will return to the three OUT signs. Turn right and make your way back to the Skimikin day use area.

TOP: *The British Columbia Skimikin Seed Orchards near Tappen.*

BOTTOM: *A gorgeous view of Skimikin Lake awaits as you return to the Skimikin Lake recreation area.*

OPPOSITE: *Granite Creek Estate Winery.*

36 Tappen Bluffs

This exhilarating, laid-back trek grants an immense panorama of Shuswap Lake's Tappen Bay at the modest cost of a gradual 331 m of elevation gain over a 4.3 km distance. This is a sensational way to squander a sunny day.

CATEGORY: Return

DISTANCE: 8.6 km round trip

HEIGHT GAIN: 331 m

HIGH POINT: 863 m

TIME: 2.5–3.5 hrs. round trip

DIFFICULTY: Moderately strenuous

SEASONS: Spring, summer, fall

TRAILHEAD COORDINATES: N50 48 40.2 W119 24 23.3

DIRECTIONS TO TRAILHEAD: On the Trans-Canada Highway westbound about 14 km west of Salmon Arm, turn left (south) onto Tappen Valley Rd. Drive 4 km and turn left on Skimikin Rd. Go 2.8 km along Skimikin Rd. to an unmarked forest service road on the right, just past the Regional District waste transfer site. A recognizable characteristic of this gravel road is that it immediately forks left and right. Park anywhere, taking care not to block traffic, as this forest service road is quite active. If you have a high-clearance vehicle, you could attempt to drive the 1.3 km to the trail, but be aware that the road is rough, with many potholes and fist-sized rocks.

The first leg of the journey consists of hiking up the gravel road for 1.3 km, while the second part exits the main road to the right onto an old, double-wide, grassy road.

1. From where you have parked and where the forest service road forks, take the left tine and begin treading upward. The hike along the road to the trail is straightforward, and even though many dirt bike and ATV tracks intersect the main road, the way is obvious. The grade flattens periodically, giving you a reprieve and also providing unobstructed viewing.

2. Once you have passed a plateaued area where the road is criss-crossed with dirt bike tracks, the trail that takes you to the bluff will be the next one on your right. Since there are no markings whatsoever, I have tied a red bandana where the trail leaves the road on the right. I hope it is left alone for a while. Red bandana or not, this departure from the main road is 1.3 km from the bottom of the road and should take 20–30 minutes of walking to achieve.

3. Once you are off the main road and onto the minor one, a cattle guard early on will confirm that you are the proper trail. The elevation gained at this point is 153 m.

4. About 10 minutes along the trail, a secondary road approaches from the left, but again the correct route is obvious. The road climbs in spots, but most of the elevation to the bluffs is accomplished toward the end of the trek.

5. Ten minutes beyond the aforementioned minor intersection, the path enters a small clearing with the bluffs in full sight straight ahead of you. The old road makes a sharp left turn and climbs upward.

6. Five minutes beyond the clearing, a very noticeable trail veers off to the right. Take this path, as it is the trail to the

summit of Tappen Bluffs. It begins climbing momentarily.

7. For the next 10 or 15 minutes, the trail meanders, seemingly lost, up and down through a pleasant forest which at times takes you away from the bluffs. However, all doubt about its destination is soon removed when you scramble very steeply for 5–10 minutes, depending on your fitness, to finally reach the bluffs.

8. The steep climb then slackens to a plateau and you arrive at the summit a few minutes later.

9. This is certainly worth the effort. The vista of Tappen Bay directly ahead and the surrounding bluffs and mountains is stunning.

TOP: *Solitude on the rarely used Tappen Bluffs Trail.*

BOTTOM: *Tappen Bay in the distance as seen from Tappen Bluffs.*

37 Balmoral Lookout Loop

This is a short trek that travels through a wondrous forest of cedar, hemlock and aspen, with views of Balmoral subdivision, Notch Hill and sprawling farmlands. This is a delightful, easy end-of-day hike.

CATEGORY: Loop

DISTANCE: 4.6 km round trip

HEIGHT GAIN: 63 m

HIGH POINT: 478 m

TIME: 1.5–2 hrs. round trip

DIFFICULTY: Moderate

SEASONS: Spring, summer, late fall

TRAILHEAD COORDINATES: N50 52 01.1 W119 21 19.5

DIRECTIONS TO TRAILHEAD: From the Trans-Canada Highway about 25 km west of downtown Salmon Arm, turn right onto Balmoral Rd. and drive 1.6 km to the Balmoral Trails parking lot.

1. The journey begins with a brief climb on a well-groomed trail, and within a couple of minutes you come to the first junction. Turn right to get on Lower South Trail.

2. A few minutes later, at the next intersection, turn right again. The grade now increases, taking you up a series of lengthy switchbacks for about five minutes.

3. After the switchbacks, the path levels, the views widen and you encounter yet another sign. At this point, Giant Tree Loop heads off to the right on an anything but giant diversion that's all of 81 m long. A fun detour to take if you want. The main trail continues straight.

4. After five minutes of level hiking, the path meets another sign, this one clearly directing you leftward to the Balmoral Viewpoint. You have now walked 1.25 km. Your options are to enjoy the view and head back down the way you came or enjoy the view and continue on an additional 3.35 km hike through a wonderful forest.

5. If you have chosen to continue, a few minutes up the trail brings you to a main intersection. Going to the right would place you on Upper South Trail to White Lake, while going left will put you on course to Blind Bay Lookout via Upper North Trail. Choose to go left. You have travelled 1.4 km.

6. Some 750 m of walking through this forest of many species brings you to a junction with a multi-purpose road. Turning right will connect you with Upper South Trail within a few short minutes.

7. Upon reaching Upper South Trail, turn right onto it and you are left with an easy 2.2 km downhill stroll to complete the loop back to the parking lot.

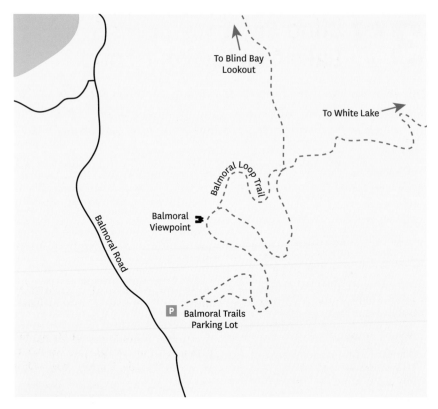

Suburbanization close to the forest's edge. A Blind Bay subdivision encroaches on the Balmoral network of trails.

38 Blind Bay to White Lake Connector

This trek is part of an intricate network of trails known as the Blind Bay/White Lake Trail System, a section of the extensive web of hiking routes maintained throughout the region by the Shuswap Trail Alliance.

Because of the elaborate array of trails in the Blind Bay/White Lake system, there is an abundance of directional signs. Although the trails are well marked, I have included directions at key junctions simply because signs can get knocked over, and without these indicators it would be difficult to find your way. If all posts are upright, simply follow the markers to White Lake.

CATEGORY: Through

DISTANCE: 16.2 km round trip

HEIGHT GAIN: 294 m

HIGH POINT: 709 m

TIME: 4 hrs. round trip

DIFFICULTY: Moderately strenuous

SEASONS: Spring, summer, early fall

TRAILHEAD COORDINATES: N50 52 01.1 W119 21 19.5

DIRECTIONS TO TRAILHEAD: From the Trans-Canada Highway approximately 25 km west of downtown Salmon Arm, turn right onto Balmoral Rd. and drive 1.6 km to the Balmoral Trails parking lot.

1. The journey begins with a brief climb on a well-groomed trail, and within a couple of minutes you meet the first junction. Turn right to get on Lower South Trail.

2. A few minutes later, at the next intersection, turn right again. The grade now increases, taking you up a series of lengthy switchbacks for about five minutes.

3. After the switchbacks, the path levels, the views widen and you encounter another sign. At this point, Giant Tree Loop heads off to the right on an optional diversion that's all of 81 m long. The main trail continues straight.

4. After five minutes of level hiking, the path meets another sign, this one directing you to the right. You have now walked 1.25 km.

5. Another 4–5 minutes of steady hiking brings you to another junction pointing to White Lake to the right.

6. With 2 km of hiking now behind you, you approach a key crossing. Once again, follow the highly visible markers to cross a multi-use road and resume on the single-track trail on the other side. You have about 6 km remaining to hike before reaching White Lake.

7. The next 1.5 km consists of a pleasant walk through an exposed mixed forest of trembling aspen and amabilis fir. The trail steepens near the end of this section, and at its zenith you will approach another major crossing. Join this multi-use trail by making a right turn, but almost immediately a minor path leaves the multi-use trail off to the left. This path is appropriately marked with signage. You now have 4.3 km remaining.

TOP: *The Blind Bay to White Lake Connector passes through a mixed forest of trembling aspen, amabilis fir, hemlock and cedar.*

BOTTOM: *The apex of the Blind Bay to White Lake Connector rewards you with a beautiful panorama of Little White Lake.*

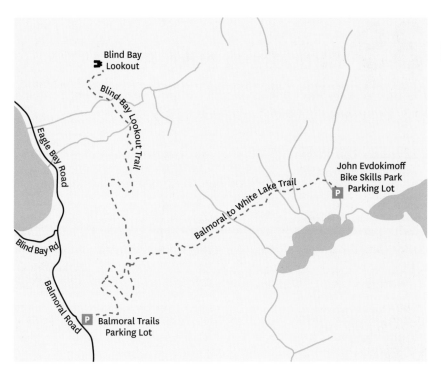

8. Ten to 15 minutes later, the path reaches its summit exposing a fantastic, unobstructed vista of Little White Lake.

9. After lingering long enough to soak in this scenery, continue along the trail as it descends to White Lake, about 3.5 km down the trail. The remainder of the journey is easily navigated as the trail criss-crosses the same multi-purpose road several times before arriving at John Evdokimoff Bike Park, approximately 45 minutes later. This bike park is the end of the trail.

10. Return the same way unless you have arranged to be picked up at the bike park.

39 Blind Bay Lookout

The trek to Blind Bay Lookout entails an arduous climb but presents spectacular views of Shuswap Lake's Blind Bay.

CATEGORY: Return

DISTANCE: 13 km round trip

HEIGHT GAIN: 417 m

HIGH POINT: 832 m

TIME: 3–3.5 hrs. round trip

DIFFICULTY: Moderately strenuous

SEASONS: Spring, summer, early fall

TRAILHEAD COORDINATES: N50 52 01.1 W119 21 19.5

DIRECTIONS TO TRAILHEAD: From the Trans-Canada Highway about 25 km west of downtown Salmon Arm, turn right onto Balmoral Rd. and drive 1.6 km to the Balmoral Trails parking lot.

1. A few minutes up the trail (about 350 m) brings you to the junction of Lower North Trail and Lower South Trail. Both routes ultimately meet up very quickly, but Lower South Trail is slightly shorter. When the paths meet again, they will place you on Ridge Trail. The grade increases for about five minutes.

2. At this point, you are following the markers to White Lake – there are no signs yet directing you to Blind Bay Lookout.

3. Soon you will come across a very brief, 81 m diversion around Giant Tree Loop. If you choose to do this little side-jaunt, it obviously won't take long.

4. A few minutes up the trail brings you to a main intersection. Choosing to go right will place you on Upper South Trail, sending you to White Lake, while choosing to go left will put you on course to Blind Bay Lookout on Upper North Trail. Choose to go left. You have travelled 1.4 km, with 5.1 remaining.

5. About 750 m of walking through this pleasant forest presents a junction with a multi-purpose road. Turn left, leaving you 4.35 km to Blind Bay Lookout.

6. This wide, grassy road lends a bit of a break before the upcoming uphill workout almost 2 km up the trail, so enjoy it while you can. During this 2 km flat walk, there are at least three markers identifying roadways into private property. The markers will guide you away from these side roads, keeping you on the appropriate route to Blind Bay Lookout. Please stay off of private property.

7. With 2.4 km remaining, a marker will direct you sharply to the left, sending you up a steep, sloped road.

8. Some 900 m, or about 20–25 minutes, later the trail plateaus as it approaches another sign, this one informing you there is 1.5 km remaining. This same sign also apprises you of a viewpoint to the left side of the road. However, this is not the summit of the climb and certainly is not Blind Bay Lookout.

9. Two hundred metres farther up the road, another sign will send you off the main road onto a single-track trail, with 1.3 km remaining. Most of this track consists of upward switchbacks, culminating on a wondrous bluff that presents an astonishing panorama of Shuswap Lake's Blind Bay. Without a doubt, this reward is worthy of your efforts.

10. Return the same way.

See map on page 141.

TOP: *Enjoy this easygoing stretch of wide, level trail, because soon you will begin climbing steadily toward Blind Bay Lookout.*

BOTTOM: *The climb to Blind Bay Lookout is worthy of your efforts, as this sensational view of Blind Bay will confirm.*

Useful websites

BC Parks
www.env.gov.bc.ca/bcparks

British Columbia Hunting & Trapping Regulations Synopsis
www.env.gov.bc.ca/fw/wildlife/hunting/regulations/

Monashee Tourism, Lumby, BC, Trail Finder
www.monasheetourism.com/Hiking-Trails.html

Regional District of Okanagan–Similkameen, Penticton, BC, Trail Search Page
http://maps.rdos.bc.ca/Html5Viewer/?viewer=rdostrails

Ribbons of Green Trails Society, Vernon, BC
www.ribbonsofgreen.ca/vernon-area-trails-maps

Shuswap Trail Alliance, Salmon Arm, BC
www.shuswaptrailalliance.com

Acknowledgements

As always, without the support and encouragement of my wife, Debbie, I would still be sitting on the couch wishing I were outside. Thank you for tolerating my weekend passion, Debbie, and thanks for your love and joy.